SO-DTC-862

The Later Years

The Later Years
Public Relations Insights
1956-1986
Edward L. Bernays

H&M PUBLISHERS

Publication date: November 22, 1986

H&M Publishers, Rhinebeck, NY 12572
© 1986 by H&M Publishers. All rights reserved.

Printed in the United States of America

Library of Congress Cataloging in Publication Data

Bernays, Edward L.
    The Later Years
    1. Public Relations

ISBN 0-9617642-0-1

Acknowledgments

Warmest thanks are due the following:

Paul Swift, managing editor, the Public Relations Quarterly, who has worked closely with the author for the past five years, for editing the text.

Richard Wambach, Wambach Communications Group, Inc., Rhinebeck, NY, art director of PRQ, for layout, type selection, cover concept.

Patricia Tate, noted Massachusetts painter, whose portrait of Edward L. Bernays reproduced on the cover is intended for the National Portrait Gallery in Washington, D.C.

—Howard Penn Hudson
Publisher

Contents

Preface

This book commemorates the unique relationship between Edward L. Bernays and the Public Relations Quarterly.

Part of it—the shorter, three-page pieces—comprises his writings as a special columnist for PRQ, under the standing head of Viewpoint, a column he began in 1976. However, he first appeared in our pages in Vol. 1, No. 2, January 1956, in an interview which represented the first time he was in print in any public relations periodical. It must be remembered that in those days he did not enjoy the popularity with the establishment which he has now. In many cases, it was quite the contrary. So it seemed natural that PRQ, as the first independent periodical in the field, should provide a forum for the creative mind of Ed Bernays. In fact, his writing intensified to the point that several years ago he undertook guest editorship of an entire issue—which one authority termed the most important single issue of any public relations magazine ever.

There are curious coincidences in our relationship. First, it covers a period of thirty years, which is a long time in the life of one person. Normally, this would occur during one's so-called peak years, 35 to 65. But in this case, our thirty-year relationship didn't start *until* Bernays was 65.

Another curious point, our relationship is marked in decades. We published my interview with him in 1956. Ten years later, 1966,

I went to his home in Cambridge and spent the day with him gathering material for our major review of his memoirs, *Biography of an Idea*. In 1976, he began his Viewpoint column in PRQ. And now, ten years later, 1986, we have this compilation of his PRQ contributions, his first book in 20 years.

My first meeting with Edward Bernays was, as one might expect, remarkable. After we had brought out the first issue of PRQ in October 1955 (then called *PR: The Quarterly Review of Public Relations*), we wanted to establish our interest in the social sciences as a basis for the practice of public relations. From what we had heard, Bernays was the main practitioner of the time who might be sympathetic to the idea. So, from Washington, D.C. I sent him a series of questions and asked that he respond to them at his convenience. A short time later I was in New York and telephoned him to see if he had my letter and what he thought. He was warm and cordial. Would I have time to come see him, he asked. The next afternoon I was at the large brownstone on the East Side which was his office.

This was a corner house, as I recall, with a large stone porch, and the bay window of his office looked out on to this porch. I was ushered into his book-lined office, and after a few minutes of amenities he called in a secretary with notebook and suggested that we get down to the interview. And interview it was, with Bernays reflecting carefully on each question, sometimes walking up and down as he answered, sometimes looking for a book on the shelves to help him make a point. Then the front door banged and I saw a well dressed woman enter the building.

Another secretary appeared with a note which Bernays studied and then he whispered to her inaudibly. Fifteen minutes later, she reappeared with another note, and again Bernays said something I couldn't hear.

I could sympathize with his dilemma, which all busy people face. I wondered whether the visitor was an important client or prospect.

I fully expected that I, a new and unknown editor, was about to be shown the door.

Ten minutes passed. Then the whole building shook as the front door shut with a tremendous bang. And the well dressed woman was on her way out. Bernays wheeled around, looked out the window at the retreating visitor and continued his sentence without breaking stride. He made no mention of the incident except, obliquely, in his farewell to me. "I've always found," he said, "that any opportunity to express one's views in print to an audience, no matter how small it may appear to be, is of the utmost importance."

In this case it certainly proved to be true: the interview was not only well received, giving impetus to our new publication, but it was also reprinted in Raymond Simon's 1966 book, *Perspectives in Public Relations,* and has since been read by generations of PR students.

In his writing and speaking he has become an impressively prolific spokesman for the profession of public relations—thus practicing what he preaches: the effectiveness of public relations. And as a practitioner, he is a superb technician.

One year, I recall, he was the opening lecturer at the New York PRSA chapter's education program. I chatted with him before he spoke. He explained that he had travelled that afternoon by train from Boston and had written out his speech during the trip. He showed me his notes on a legal pad.

After the lecture, I went to my apartment and opened my mail. I found a press release from Bernays, mailed two days before from Cambridge, giving me the highlights of the talk which he said he had just written that afternoon. Then it dawned on me. The trick was to write the release first, to emphasize the news points. And from the release he prepared the formal presentation, knowing that the talk would have the newsworthy points up front.

The final remarkable coincidence of this relationship between PRQ and Edward Bernays is Marvin Olasky, professor of journalism at the University of Texas, and our newest contributing editor. In earlier times I knew all of the major academics in the public relations field, and many have been active in the pages of PRQ. Marvin Olasky I have yet to meet, but I am an admirer. I have judged him by what he writes and how he writes it. And he, in turn, has made his own judgment of Edward L. Bernays, which he has shared with readers of PRQ in his 1984 article, "Roots of Modern Public Relations: The Bernays Doctrine."

So I am able to end this thirty-year account of an impressive man not in my words, but in those of a contemporary scholar who is carrying on the task which both Edward Bernays and the Public Relations Quarterly value so much: thoughtful research and writing about public relations. Olasky concludes: "Bernays saw a wider role of public relations in a confused civilization. Current practitioners should study his work so that they may embrace it and extend their awareness of the deeper meaning of what they do, or reject it and reach for alternatives."

—Howard Penn Hudson
Editor and Publisher
Public Relations Quarterly
Fall 1986

The Later Years

What Do the Social Sciences Have to Offer Public Relations?

An Interview with Edward L. Bernays
by Howard Penn Hudson

Presented here is the verbatim transcript of an interview given the Editor in Mr. Bernays' office in New York on December 8, 1955. Because of space limitations some portions have been omitted.

HPH: *Mr. Bernays, in many of your writings you have alluded to the social sciences as being the source of knowledge upon which future developments of the public relations field will depend. Do you think that the social sciences have already made important contributions to public relations?*

ELB: I think we should define the terms social sciences and public relations before we discuss the subject. Public relations, as I interpret it, is a field of activity which has to do with the interaction between an individual, a group, an idea, or other unit with the publics on which it depends. A counsel on public relations is an expert who advises on relations with these publics. He attempts to define the socially sound objectives of his client or project. He attempts to find out by research what the adjustments or maladjustments are between his client and the publics on which he depends. He advises his client, first, to modify its patterns of behavior, its attitudes, to conform to public demands, so that the client may reach the goals agreed upon. When the client's procedures have been adjusted where necessary, he then advises on how to give the public a better understanding of the client. Since we live in a competitive society, the public relations man tries to persuade these publics to accept the client's point of view or product.

Public relations covers the relations of a man, institution, idea, with its publics. Any efficient attempt to improve these relations depends on our understanding of the behavioral sciences and applying them—sociology, social psychology, anthropology, history, etc. The social sciences are the foundation of public relations. If the behavioral sciences have made any contribution to our knowledge of behavior, it is obvious that a knowledge of them is basic to a consultant, who tries to improve the relations between an individual, group, or idea and the public.

In a recent study, Rensis Likert, Director of the Institute for Social Research of the University of Michigan, on Public Relations and the Social Sciences, points out that social science knowledge is applied in adjusting the relations of supervisors to employees, to other aspects of industrial relations. Through an understanding of psychology and social psychology, it was possible to define these relationships and show how they might be improved.

To show how important social scientists are to public relations, here is an example of recognition of their importance, even though distorted. There is widespread emphasis today on so-called motivation. There is an unfounded belief in promotion and advertising fields that the answer to the secret of "motivation" will automatically solve all problems. This idea obviously ignores many other factors affecting behavior. Social pressures at any moment may change any answers that this type of incomplete research into motivation may have given us. Factors affecting individual personality may change the results of motivation research. Memory and retention values may be more important than motivation. Many other factors play a part in the cross-currents of behavior in addition to motivation. I point to this example to stress how important it is in dealing with the social sciences not to let fads, gimmicks, and distortions due to half-knowledge control us.

In public relations, too much emphasis has been placed on the concept of attitudes as a basis of action rather than on the broad concept of human behavior as a whole. The complex field of behavior takes in all aspects of behavior in life, as far as we have studied them and know them. This obviously is complicated. Many of us still take the easy road, thinking of humans as single-tracked individuals with attitudes that can be titillated to give Pavlovian responses in our directions.

HPH: *Which disciplines of the social sciences do you think are most important to us in public relations?*

ELB: This is a tough question to answer. It's as tough as expecting a physician to give an answer to the question of whether blood chemistry, physics of joint movements, or human physiology are most important to him. The importance of any special social science field to the public relations practitioner of necessity depends on the specific problem. In communications, one segment of the field, we deal with a complex of areas of social sciences, from public opinion, social psychology and individual psychology, to economics.

In problems concerned with relations between supervisor and personnel, we draw on social and individual psychology, and communications plays a part too.

In a problem of business policy in relation to publics, we draw on broader fields of knowledge.

How to adjust the brewing industry to the people after Prohibition? To handle this intelligently demands a knowledge of the historical pattern of the behavior of the American people towards sumptuary law. We need to know something about the social history of our country, of community and individual behavior in different parts of the country. Cultural anthropology may be important for us, too.

In a problem of adjusting employee relationships in a community in which there are many different racial stocks of Americans, sociology and anthropology may be important disciplines to guide us in our activity.

HPH: *Could you give some examples of the manner in which these various fields have contributed to public relations?*

ELB: It is difficult to isolate them in terms of contribution. Just as difficult as it would be for a physician who operated on your appendix to name the areas of medicine which contributed to the success of the operation. He might say, with equal truth—a study of the skin, of the blood circulatory system, of the healing qualities of time, of the relationship of the chemical action of antibiotics to possible infection.

When you deal with a problem in public relations, whether it be the problem of getting the American people better adjusted to the health-giving value of bananas, or getting the American people to accept the principle of the eight-hour day, pensions or guaranteed employment, you often deal with many separate fields of social science that impinge on the situation. If you are to advise on public relations aspects of guaranteed employment, you must understand the history of the labor movement in America and its importance to capitalism. You must understand the attitude of its great religions towards men and towards work. It may be well to know what happened in other countries as well. When you deal with politics, you impinge on social psychology and individual psychology. You must, for instance, understand the workings of the authoritarian personality which has been clearly defined in terms of its insecurities and inferiorities. You must know something about the psychopathology of politics, and something about the mainsprings of the American tradition.

In the 20th century, the universities in this country laid stress on studying human behavior. The trends that pervaded the late 19th century and early 20th century in Europe as well as in this country furthered social science study. The work of European sociologists and psychologists, and the work in this country of people at the University of Chicago, Columbia, Harvard, and others accelerated this, so that today, according to statistics, there are 30,000 men and women engaged in the study of human behavior.

It is a great shame that with all the knowledge available, there should still be the great gap between the thinkers and the doers in our country. So little of the knowledge available is applied for constructive social ends. In our early history in this country, the thinkers and doers were one and the same people. Jefferson was a thinker and a doer. So was Benjamin Franklin, and James Madison. As a result of different trends the gap between thinker and doer has widened. I think this occurred in the 1875-1900 period, when rugged individualists without much education amassed great amounts of money. To show their prowess they practiced conspicuous waste and conspicuous consumption. To justify their own power they looked down on thinkers. This attitude caused the attack on Roosevelt's "brain trust," the attack on Stevenson's "double domes" and "egg-heads," and on "long-hairs" generally. The doer who had carved out the wilderness and harnessed rapids for power had to justify his own position against the power of the brains who, after all, were useless in a society which needed wood-cutters and bear-hunters.

Today, of course, we are dealing in a highly complex society in which the sciences, both physical and social, are our hope of survival and of growth as well. There is today, fortunately, a better rapprochement between the doer and the *physical* scientists; very little as yet between the doer and the *social* scientist. It is easier to get a company to hire a new physicist than it is to get it to hire a cultural anthropologist even though the anthropologist may be more important for that company.

HPH: *What about some examples of ways in which you have used the social sciences to solve practical public relations problems?*

ELB: Here are some examples:

a. Depth analysis on the use of leather soles showed that leather was associated with the status of the individual from childhood on. Childhood conditioning, it was learned, played an important part in people's attitude toward leather. This knowledge could be used in promoting leather soles.

b. When radios were first made they had little status. They were inexpensive "jalopies." And the radio stations and networks geared their programs to lower socio-economic groups. The problem of the radio manufacturer was to develop new values for radio so that radio would appeal to all America. It was found this could be done by organizing a Radio Institute of the Audible Arts, which carried on nationwide educational activities to develop public understanding and support of the radio as an important social value in our society. This in turn raised the standard of programs on the radio. Radio networks recognized they were getting to a higher socio-economic audience.

c. The American public, in keeping with American Protestant tradition, needs to rationalize its pleasures really to enjoy them. They may enjoy a fruit, but might not eat as much because they like it so much. In projecting this fruit for greater acceptance, it is important to find in it some useful values that will give the individual who enjoys it a reason additional to his enjoyment, for eating it. Many of the important fruit-growers' organizations have learned this and have applied it, as, for instance, orange growers and packers who have stressed vitamins quite properly and thus have accelerated the market.

d. A manufacturer of trains for children knows that he is advertising not only to children but also the infantilism of the fathers of children. That is why you often see a father in an advertisement of toy trains.

HPH: *Do you think knowledge of the social sciences is a requisite for success in public relations?*

ELB: The answer is if users of public relations services were aware of the importance of these sciences, they would know that command of social sciences is requisite to success. But employers of

Edward L. Bernays

Howard Penn Hudson

the public relations adviser are possibly just as ignorant of the needs of the field as many practitioners are themselves.

Knowledge of the social sciences under present day conditions is not a prerequisite to success in the profession. However, when, as and if those spending the money for public relations understood the potential of these skills, social science will be a requisite just as it is required that a physician have a medical degree from an accredited institution before he may practice his profession.

Before the Flexner Report on medical education in 1910, thousands of doctors were practicing in the United States who had received their degrees from mail order diploma mills. Success as a medical quack depended only on whether he could get away with ignorance or whether he was found out.

HPH: *Are you satisfied with the present liaison between the social sciences and public relations? Have adequate provisions been made for public relations to benefit from the social sciences?*

ELB: My answer is "No" to the first half of the question, due to no one's fault except what the sociologists call the "cultural time lag." The social scientist is still rather remote from the field of the practice of public relations. The public relations man is even more remote from the field of the social scientist. There are social scientists who write about public relations. However, few public relations specialists have gone deeply into the social sciences or written about them.

Very few, if any, provisions have been made for public relations to benefit from the social sciences. I know of no joint committees of public relations men and social scientists that represent a liaison, although it is possible that some of the numerous public relations societies that have cropped up may have them. There are, of course, numerous ways in which a public relations practitioner can avail himself of social science information. There are learned journals in many fields, from the *Australian Journal of Applied Social Sciences* to the *Journal of Applied Anthropology,* etc. And the public relations man can join numerous learned societies such as the Society for the Psychological Study of Social Issues.

There are bibliographical aids and helps, such as monthly abstracts of sociology. But there are no joint committees functioning to discuss mutual problems.

HPH: *How can a busy practitioner keep up-to-date on developments in the social sciences?*

ELB: There are three good ways I know. The first is to be a busy reader, to look through whatever may have any value in gaining new knowledge. I have no sympathy with the man who says he has no time to read. A busy man has no time to neglect reading. Reading is quicker than learning through trial and error. In that connection, bibliographies are short cuts to reading the most needful literature.

A second way is to keep track of the field by reading popular treatments of the disciplines. There are, for instance, such books as *Outside Readings in Psychology,* and *Readings in Social Psychology,* which survey the field and help a man to explore it further if there should be occasion to do so. There are bibliographies; for instance, the Harvard University *Annotated Bibliography of Books of Psychology.* And then there are popularizations such as those of Stuart Chase. Books are basic to knowledge. If you go into any situation with only what you know from personal experience you are obviously not as well off as if you go into it with facts and points of view of specialists.

Another way, of course, is to know men in the social science field, themselves aware of the developments in the public relations field. Personal contact can keep you in touch with the field.

HPH: *How do you think we could make social scientists more aware of the needs of public relations?*

ELB: Social scientists generally are already aware of public relations. They have shown that in their comments in books and pamphlets. They have brought out extensive bibliographies on public opinion and propaganda. One example, a recent issue of *Human Organization,* published by the Society for Applied Anthropology, discusses the businessman and the social sciences, indicates an awareness of the problem, and shows what is being done in the field.

However, that awareness by sensitive academicians has not produced action because stepping out from academic circles into practical life is not usually practicable. Some organizations have taken a first step—the Association for the Psychological Study of Social Issues, made up of social psychologists, is a relatively recent organization. The Society for Social Studies is equally new. So is the Society for Applied Anthropology. These societies try to apply their disciplines by translating them into action. But, compared to the activities of any Chamber of Commerce, these societies still have a lot of bridges to build.

What the situation demands is that more public relations men with a feeling for and understanding of social science should help bring theory and practice together. That is already being accomplished in individual cases. Obviously, one way to make social scientists more aware of the needs of public relations is not to tackle the problem in terms of the needs of public relations, but rather in terms of how both groups can work together for the common goals of society. I think any social science organization would today welcome the cooperation of any honorable public relations man if it is understood that he is not merely self-interested in the relationship.

There are still many who deplore social science and put their emphasis on common sense, as if common sense could solve the problems of mankind. It hasn't done so since the time of the Neanderthal man. And still the common sense approach is prevalent.

HPH: *Admittedly there are successful public relations practitioners today who see little benefit in the social sciences. They say we need more practical "how to do it" information rather than* *"theory." Would you comment?*

ELB: To me all such objections are poppycock. The fact that we have not as yet a cure for the common cold in no way disproves the importance of the findings of science as to the human body and germs. The fact that we have not as yet the answer to cancer control or cure is no derogation of the scientific approach to cancer control. It seems to me we must accept this basic fact, that individual behavior can be studied just as well as the behavior of things. A scientific approach is basic to any understanding of a world as complex as the one we live in. To use the findings of the social scientists is to proceed with the available knowledge in this field, comparable to what we do so effectively in the physical sciences which has not, as yet, been able to produce protoplasm. Just as Einstein found the equation that led to atomic fission, we may hope for social scientists who will develop formulae for social fusion.

There is one footnote to be made to this, however. Just as the social scientists have found that certain tribes of Indians in Central America eat certain plants without knowing why they do so, which plants later on were found to have ingredients lacking in their ordinary diet, so it is undoubtedly true that many common sense steps undoubtedly have a much more basic reason.

But certainly it is sounder to know scientifically why one is doing something than to do it by rote or by gosh, because our ancestors did it.

HPH: *Here is a general question. Recently there have been a number of reports and studies attempting to describe the kind of world we shall live in in 1975. What do you think the practice of public relations will be like twenty years from now?*

ELB: We initiated the professional practice of public relations in 1920, which is almost the same time period in point of the past as 1975 is in the future. In *Crystallizing Public Opinion* (written in 1923) we foresaw the practice of public relations as it is now being carried on. But it did not envisage the technological improvements in communications which have accelerated these processes. It is equally difficult to encompass the technological speed-ups in transportation and communication that might transform the physical world, from jet planes to television on telephones, and to whatever may follow these processes. That must be left to the imagination of the science fiction writers.

If our society continues to function in a democratic way through change and adjustment, through accommodation of varying groups and viewpoints of one with another, through progress at uneven rates of the constituent elements that make up society, there will be even greater necessity than there is today for a public relations practitioner. He will be helpful in evaluating the adjustments and maladjustments between the groups that make up the society, will advise his clients or employers on their attitudes and actions, will help them achieve their goals, and will interpret client or employer organization to the publics concerned.

Such a man will need training in the social sciences.

He will go through an apprenticeship or internship in some establishment before practicing.

He will be licensed by the state as to character, ability, and training. Society will hardly want to risk the dangerous tampering the effective practitioner will be in a position to do, without such licensing.

He will reap the social and monetary rewards an individual of such qualifications receives from society.

If, on the other hand, our society moves to statism of the right or the left and there is no room for the normal processes of flexibility of a democratic society, there will be no such vocation.

The future of the public relations man is linked up with the future of a free society.

Winter 1956

ELB in Puerto Rico with Madam Munoz Marin, widow of Luis Munoz Marin, who was instrumental in establishing Puerto Rico as a Commonwealth of the U.S. Bernays assisted Munoz Marin in the early fifties in helping him win that status. He visited the island again in 1985 as a guest of Fernando Valverde, president of the Public Relations Society of Puerto Rico, and its members.

Steps Toward an Adequate U.S. Overseas Information Program

Recent demonstrations against the United States in Paris, Beirut, Rangoon, Jakarta, Algiers, Tokyo and South America have focused intense public interest on the overseas information activities of the United States. Many in and out of government are reappraising the program's part in our foreign relations.

Four years ago some thirty of us in the public opinion field formed a committee to advance America's overseas information program. We chose the name "National Committee for an Adequate Overseas U.S. Information Program." Admittedly cumbersome, it described our intentions. The word "adequate," particularly, conveyed the difficulties the U.S. faces in its overseas information program. Realistically, we could work only for an "adequate" program. This limitation stems from the nature of our free, highly developed, democratic society and from other causes. Many complex and diverse problems must be solved if we are to make progress—problems semantic, historical, ideological, practical, technological, organizational, political, economic, human and otherwise.

With all the difficulties, I am surprised we are doing as well as we are—a by-no-means adequate performance. Only a revolution in the thinking and action of the American people will improve those aspects of the operation which can be improved. Nothing should be permitted to stand in the way of such improvement. An examination of the problems may help the American people to understand them better and to make a start toward betterment.

Problem Number One

Problem number one deals with semantics. We call the activity "overseas information." We do not mean overseas information alone. We mean a program to influence people's opinions and attitudes in support of the United States through the planned distribution of facts and ideas. Congress and the executive branch of the government in the last decades have not come to grips with this reality behind the nomenclature.

Uncertainty about nomenclature has prevailed since the Committee on Public Information first undertook such activity in World War I. In World War II, as in World War I, despite vital national need, odium attached to those who did this work. When later we adopted propaganda as a peacetime effort, as a normal part of our U.S. diplomatic relations and foreign policy, we still had compunctions about the ethics and propriety of trying to influence foreign peoples, and whether our government should use a weapon nowhere mentioned in the Constitution. We assuaged our sense of guilt by calling what we did information. Giving out factual truth or information was part of the democratic doctrine. It relieved us of moral responsibility in trying to influence other people. Yet social science has found that one man's truth may be another man's untruth.

For our national purpose facts are only facts and truth is only truth when they are accepted by others. Of course, we as a nation must be concerned in using only truth. But to make the truth meaningful and acceptable to those to whom it is projected, we must use it effectively. Fuzziness exists as to what this instrumentality we call U.S. overseas information really is. The Administration, Congress, the Agency and our people are obfuscated about the operation. Those at whom we aim our activities are aware of its purposes.

What Should Be Accomplished?

A second problem is overcoming ignorance of the Administration, Congress and the people as to what such activity can accomplish. Often accomplishments are expected that are outside its scope. In 1954 a report of the Royal Commission of Enquiry into the Overseas Information Services of Great Britain assessed the actual and potential value of overseas information. Its conclusions, based on the sheer weight of evidence, found overseas information played an *essential* role in the foreign policy of England and other great powers. The Commission said, ". . . a modern government has to concern itself with public opinion abroad and be properly equipped to deal with it . . . information services must today be regarded as part of the normal apparatus of diplomacy of a great power." It pointed out that "propaganda is no substitute for policy or for military strength, economic efficiency or financial stability" and that it is as easy to underrate the potentialities of such a program as to overrate them. The effect on the course of events of such a program is never likely to be more than marginal, it said, but "may be decisive in tipping the balance between diplomatic success and failure."

These conclusions, yet unrecognized by many of our policy makers, apply with equal force to our own overseas information services. At Congressional appropriations hearings a Congressman will ask why money is needed for activity in a country where the U.S. position has deteriorated. Overseas information is not regarded as a normal continuing function of foreign relations. It is often thought of only as an ad hoc innovation to fight Communism in the cold war.

Increased Support

A third problem is how to increase Congressional and our people's support. Congress' support is proportionate to the people's, a truism of representative government. Our young country places reliance on material strength, neglecting reliance on ideas, in international relations as in education. Ignorance, suspicion, skepticism and fear of overseas information intensify this negative attitude. Our experience has conditioned us to abhor propaganda: the German prior to World War I, the Communist of the Bolsheviks during and after World War I, Hitler's world-wide propaganda, Mussolini's fascist, Japanese co-existence propaganda in World War II, and the ever-rising tides of Communist propaganda today. We are concerned lest our own government use this tool to try to control the minds of men here. We fear the possibility of a breakdown of the competition of ideas in the democratic market place of ideas, though we don't seem to mind commercial advertising propaganda.

Our moralistic viewpoint that propaganda is not truth militates against our support of the overseas information program. And we cannot understand why there should be one Voice of America when our tradition always calls for many voices.

People who support an overseas information program often do so for the wrong reasons—that people overseas become our friends if they know us better; that the more we communicate, the better the results; that information serves the function of persuasion; and that gifts make friends.

A fourth problem is that of making our national policymaking leaders more aware of the importance of shaping their foreign policy deeds in ways to affect foreign attitudes favorably. The propaganda impact of the substance, timing and method of government foreign policy is important. What our government does is always more important than what it says. A goodwill tour that turns into an ill will tour is unsound foreign policy and poor propaganda.

A fifth problem is to make Americans aware that what happens in this country shapes attitudes of foreigners toward us. Foreign policy begins at home. We as a nation are judged by the attitudes and acts of our people in relation to the national ideals we profess. News flashed to the world of an Indian ambassador mistreated in a Texan airport because of his color or a Pakistanian diplomatic corps member arrested as a gypsy in a Westchester suburb may be more potent in conditioning foreign attitudes than foreign policy statements of a Secretary of State. Little Rock, a *Confidential* trial, and bombings of Negro homes and Jewish synagogues in the South play their parts in our losing prestige in other parts of the world.

A sixth problem is determination of the content of our messages. We must know what we want to communicate. What is the America we want to project? Is it the America of the conservative or progressive; of long-hair artists or of comics and rock and roll; is it urban or rural; technological or idealistic? How should our unresolved controversial issues be treated, whether of reciprocal trade treaties or international policy? And what criteria should govern content that may be critical of the Administration in office, Congress or other powerful interests? Granted the program is nonpartisan and objective, by what criteria are ideas and facts to be chosen and presented from the welter of ideas around us? Multiple truths vie for attention. Which shall be selected? Research may answer the question as to the kind of information that has impact and on whom. We still have to decide on content policy. Certainly, dynamic ideas like those of Thomas Jefferson, Woodrow Wilson and other great American leaders have a place on any program. And it is obvious that the organization carrying out policy should be independent, free of politics, red tape and bureaucracy.

A Balanced Picture of the U.S.

A seventh problem is shaping the program to present a balanced picture of the U.S. Most people get their image of the United States through private commercial communications channels. News media, American and foreign, radio and press, present us to the world in symbols that do not necessarily present a balanced image. A deviant happening in Kentucky or Wyoming may, through distribution by wire, radio, mail or word of mouth, affect our country's reputation in Iraq. Unofficial voices from America constantly affect the changing image the minds of men get of us—movies, books, comics, our products wherever used, over a million tourists a year abroad, a half-million American residents abroad, and the members of our government personnel abroad, military and civilian. The members of the foreign diplomatic corps here and the impression of America that foreign students and travellers bring back to their homelands affect our prestige. Activities of American private overseas information agencies play a part: Radio Free Europe to satellite countries and Radio Liberation into Russia. Any official U.S. agency has the almost impossible task of trying to keep the image of the U.S. well defined and balanced, in competition with these myriad other impacts on foreign people, but without duplication.

An eighth problem is that of resolving competition of official propagandas of our allies with our program. No coordinated approach has been worked out between our official Agency and those of our friends. At times, when there is a difference of policy between us and our allies, we may become the target.

Obtaining Qualified Personnel

A ninth problem is how to get the best possible personnel into the Agency, from administrator down through the ranks. Administrators have been appointed who were not the best qualified men available for the job. Men from advertising, news magazines, diplomacy, higher education and the business side of broadcasting have headed the program. Naturally, they did the best they could.

Often it was not good enough. No one may be the perfect man and have all the requisite qualifications. But certainly a lifetime of executive and administrative practice in the arts of persuasion would appear to be a prerequisite. He should certainly be an intellectual with respect for the social sciences—cultural anthropology, sociology, public opinion, etc. He should certainly be versed in foreign affairs, a diplomat and politician in the broadest sense. He must be imaginative and courageous. The Administrator is not always chosen because of his fitness for the job.

Equally difficult problems are involved with the ten thousand individuals in the organization. Status and tenure are uncertain today. There is no independent career service. Many staff members have only limited qualifications. A recent report of the U.S. Advisory Commission on Information states: "... certain areas are understaffed while others may well be overstaffed. Greater critical attention should be given to the Agency's personnel policies and practices, as well as to the quality and quantity of the personnel itself." The report finds weaknesses in training, particularly in language training. "The Commission strongly re-states its belief in the necessity for a long-range training program for Agency personnel." Practical-minded administrators shy away from "intellectuals" and do not harness the knowledge of social scientists and of area and communications experts to the activity.

The Role of Research

A tenth problem is research. In this pioneering work, continuing thorough research into area and political conditions, human behavior and output is a prerequisite. A pig in a poke is no international bargain. Research can help define the Agency activities, what we say, whom it reaches, under whose auspices it should be said. Research can help define the nature of the best interpersonal contacts, the tone of the message, the part the fight against communism should play, the media to be used and the program's effectiveness. Research can help define the assumptions on which the Agency proceeds. We must be sure the assumptions on which we are working are proven assumptions, if possible, and that all work in accord with them. At present in the Agency many staff members often make their own assumptions without regard to their proven validity. If there were comprehensive research, the Agency and thousands of people in it would know that the assumptions they were working on were valid.

Some research is carried on. The program, social scientists maintain, calls for much more comprehensive research.

Policies decided on after research should be clearly stated and made applicable to all people in the Agency concerned with them. When there is inadequate research, consistency in practice should prevail.

Needed New Facilities

Problem eleven is providing adequate physical facilities for the transmission of our messages. Needed facilities in radio include the improvement of present equipment and additional facilities, to meet Communist propaganda efforts. Television facilities and activities need long-range expansion, so essential in the envisioned world-wide TV communications network. According to the latest U.S. Advisory Commission on Information report, "... the Agency has been unable to develop an imaginative and constructive TV program" and "... to use effectively a powerful new medium that is gradually spreading around the world, namely, TV."

Problem twelve is how a democratic overseas information activity can most effectively counter the monolithic propaganda of Soviet Russia. Their attacks on us are based on falsifications, distortion and deception. Their accusations confuse the world and weaken our prestige.

Totalitarian Soviet Russia coordinates deeds and words at top level to carry out national policy. The Central Committee of the

Russian Communist Party works with Agitprop, the planning group immediately beneath it. Foreign policy and propaganda programs are decided on to affect the attitudes and actions of people throughout the world. Soviet Russia adds censorship, a controlled press, lies and double-dealing as instruments of national policy.

How Communists Function

Communist parties and Communist fronts carry forward the Communist line on a world-wide basis, among them 40 international front organizations, including trade unions, teachers', lawyers', scientists' and women's groups. Many publications, newspapers, picture magazines, books are sold at low prices; exhibits and trade fairs are held. Travels of artists, scientists and technical experts propagandize the Communist doctrine. Soviet Russia is run as a propaganda apparatus, with 375,000 propagandists full time, according to a Senate Foreign Relations Committee report; with 2,100,000 part-time propagandists and with 7,000 Soviet newspapers as part of the domestic machinery. The budget is estimated to be several billion dollars. This is tough competition, aided by economic penetration and political subversion and other weapons in the cold war.

Problem thirteen is how to assure the U.S. an enlarged, stable and continuing budget to cope with its overseas needs. Some experts believe the budget should be a billion dollars, ten times the present amount spent. A billion dollars is a small sum for the insurance values such a program offers. One company, Unilever, spent £83,000,000, approximately $232,000,000 in advertising last year, communicating with 1,800,000,000 consumers in the free world. We are trying to reach about 1,000,000,000 more people.

Congress does not reflect a continuing planned informed approach in appropriating funds. A timid administration that fears the antagonism of individual Congressmen may lower its budgetary requests, beyond a necessary minimum. A Senator McCarthy makes the Agency a whipping boy and can cripple it for a time.

Present Size of USIA

The Congress appropriated some $100 million last year for the United States Information Agency. It has 10,000 personnel, with information missions in 79 countries and a total of 193 information service posts; 155 Information Centers in 64 countries; 77 Binational Centers in 25 countries; radio transmitters at 7 locations in the United States and at 10 overseas locations; motion pictures— about 1,100 program films in USIS film libraries; 2,542,275 books in USIS libraries, of which 1,764,191 are in English and 778,084 in translations; 22 bookmobiles; 68 magazines or editions of magazines produced abroad—18 in English and 50 in foreign languages. The Agency also produces two English and one foreign language publications in the United States for overseas use. The Agency has complete radio teletype facilities at 79 posts for receiving the Agency's wireless file; and has 225 exhibits of a permanent nature. With these resources, human and mechanical, it is trying to do a job in the broader frame of reference we have outlined.

The conduct of our foreign policy is so complex that no one individual, no matter how potent, can effect overnight change to solve the solvable problems.

In a democracy, fortunately, this condition is subject to change if public understanding and support can be aroused. Public understanding and support is a prerequisite to an adequate U.S. overseas information program. We know the thoughts and actions that guide our people in respect to overseas information cannot be changed overnight. We need public reorientation. That takes time. But enlightened men and women can help improve the situation.

A First Step

As a first step, they can urge Congressional hearings by the Senate Foreign Relations or the House Foreign Affairs Committee to give public visibility to the issue to develop serious understanding of the issue. Experts would give testimony on the scope and function of the Agency and the problems it faces. Then democratic processes would be put in motion to cope with them.

A great voluntary national group comparable to the American Association for the Advancement of Science might arise from such hearings to support a continuing educational and information program.

Other voluntary bodies, like the Foreign Policy Association, The League of Women Voters, World Affairs Councils could be enlisted to use the great channels of public information and education to inform and educate the public and its leaders.

Nationwide interest would resolve many of the problems discussed. The semantic difficulties would be clarified. The objective would be defined to the Administration, Congress and the people alike. The support of Congress and the people would be ensured. Policy makers in their foreign policy actions would give greater attention to propaganda considerations. We would learn that foreign policies begin at home. Content of a program would be defined as a result of debate and discussion.

Use of Private Channels

The ideas, news and facts that flow from America to other countries through private channels would, of course, continue. More balanced presentation should result from heightened responsibility of media. There would be little difficulty in cooperation and adjustment with friendly countries. Public understanding and support should ensure that organization and execution of information, policy and strategy is at a high level. Recognition of program importance should trade on the personnel of the Agency. Educational facilities to train recruits and ensure them adequate rewards, status and tenure would be stimulated. Social scientists would participate in such a program.

Public understanding would ensure from Congress enlarged budgets, continuous and stable, and the provision of enlarged technological facilities. And we would have a more potent and efficient organization to meet false Soviet promises and pronouncements.

An official United States overseas information agency is vital under today's and tomorrow's foreseeable world. Problems to be overcome will not be solved quickly or completely. The Agency's effectiveness will always depend on how sound our national policies are. International persuasion is only one of the instruments of national policy. It must be coordinated with the highest policies and actions of our government. If international persuasion were based on clearly defined, sound national policy and backed by Congress and the people, results would obviously be more effective. Everyone interested in our survival can play a part in stimulating the public and private action to bring this about.

Summer 1958

Barbara Brilliant, director of her own television program on WBZ, NBC station in Boston, with ELB, who participated as guest on her show in 1985.

Biography of an Idea: Memoirs of Public Relations Counsel Edward L. Bernays

Simon and Schuster, New York, 1965, 849 pp., $12.95.

Reviewed by Howard Penn Hudson.

It was to be expected that the first public relations practitioner to publish his memoirs at length would be Edward L. Bernays. One of the prolific writers in the field starting with his landmark *Crystallizing Public Opinion* in 1923, he has written so widely that there even exists a printed bibliography issued in 1950. Mr. Bernays has obviously decided to make this book a crowning achievement and in that he has succeeded.

We have become used to famous lawyers and doctors writing their memoirs, thus establishing themselves in the public mind as interesting people in vital professions. Up until now, the public has had no occasion to really know a public relations man. And such books that have been written by public relations leaders have related primarily to their work, with little suggestion of their personalities.

Edward L. Bernays breaks this barrier. His long career with well known people, his involvement in important social and economic and political issues, gives him the basic material that makes this book much more than a description of public relations techniques. By revealing himself as a warm person, with strong opinions about the issues of his times—by setting down intimate observations about famous persons as widely different as Caruso, Freud and Coolidge—he conveys to the public the nature of public relations. Moreover, he shows public relations at work for the benefit of social causes, the arts, health and welfare, in addition to serving business.

It is a sign of the coming of age of public relations when a publisher thinks a public relations practitioner's life story is worth printing. *Biography of an Idea* is a fascinating social history of the past fifty years, as well as a first rate autobiography.

Bernays himself has often been controversial. A "loner" who never joined a professional public relations group, he has won the dislike if not the enmity of various of his colleagues. He himself once boasted that one public relations luncheon club fined any member who mentioned the name Bernays. It is natural, therefore, that this book has already produced intense feelings as we have learned in discussing it with other professionals. Some have said that there are gross inaccuracies that cannot be attributed to a normal distortion of memory. (His claim that he developed the soap-sculptor movement for Ivory soap is just one statement that has been disputed.) Others have objected to the revelation of client relationships as being unethical. Regardless, as in the recent Kennedy books, it certainly makes for good reading. And in public relations particularly, there is far too little in print about what really goes on.

Early History

Certainly this book shows how little is known about the history of public relations. We are still in the stage of dealing with the history makers. And until more is known about Ivy Lee, Arthur Page, Carl Byoir, John Hill, Pendleton Dudley, Paul Garrett, to name just a few, we do not have the documentation that a historian needs to pull the story together. Perhaps a characteristic of public relations men is their lack of interest in the history of their field. Meanwhile, anything that is set down on paper by the pioneers is adding to our heritage.

Unless the reader has some historical perspective he is going to be misled by descriptions of techniques used by Bernays in his early campaigns. Now part of regular practice and hence familiar to practitioners, they were largely unknown and untested in the early period in which Bernays practiced. In the life story of one man, then, we can trace the development of much of what we now know as the practice of public relations.

A favorite device of researchers in public relations is to survey the educational backgrounds of practitioners and then present the findings as guidance for educating for the future. Such surveys usually show that the preponderance of practitioners took either journalism or liberal arts courses. Once more, Bernays is unique. He studied agriculture! But there is no desire on his part to advocate such a curriculum. He rushed through his courses, graduated early, and notes that "My three and a half years at Cornell University College of Agriculture gave me little stimulation and less learning . . . it furnished in a negative way a test for aptitudes and adjustments. It proved I was unsuited temperamentally for the rural life and was city minded."

But if Bernays did not then know what he wanted to do, he quickly recognized it when it came along. An early job was with a medical journal. A more prosaic mind might have been content with simply doing the job at hand. But it wasn't long before

Bernays had stumbled onto a play "Damaged Goods," which discussed syphilis, an unheard of thing on the stage of 1913, had organized a citizens committee, got the play launched on Broadway, sent it to Washington for a performance before President Wilson and his Cabinet, and obtained international publicity.

The success of this venture led him directly into press representation for other Broadway plays, then into the opera, the ballet and the handling of a tour for Caruso. Unable to qualify for the armed services, Bernays got an assignment with the U.S. Committee on

ELB, Cornell University B.S. graduate, 1912, greeted in 1986 by members of the Cornell chapter of Public Relations Student Society in Ithaca, N.Y.

Public Information, popularly known as the Creel Committee, and this in turn led him to the Peace Conference in Paris after the war, in which another pioneer of public relations, Carl Byoir, also participated. And when he returned to New York to re-start his career, he took on a special assignment for Byoir for the Lithuanian National Council of the United States.

With the contacts he had developed in these early years, Bernays launched his own office and within a year had ten employees. The story that then enfolds in abundance tells of his work with clients, a wide range which included big business, social groups like the NAACP, and periodic assignments for the government. He describes how, when suddenly pressed for a statement on what he really did, he coined the phrase "public relations counsel"—how he decided to put down on paper a fuller explanation which resulted in his book *Crystallizing Public Opinion* and how he further, in 1923, started to teach public relations at New York University.

Techniques of Self Promotion

It is clear that Bernays had an instinctive knowledge of the value and the techniques of self promotion. Just as an ambitious young lawyer joins every civic and political movement available, so did Bernays take on all assignments which would call attention to himself. Late in the twenties his house in Greenwich Village became something of a salon for celebrities in all kinds of endeavors, and so his fame spread. Both by his own descriptions and statements from others, Bernays has always displayed the characteristics of utter self-confidence. He was not a behind-the-scenes technician, but always aimed to be a person in his own right and with strong social and economic and political viewpoints.

This book is much more than one man's story, however. It is an interesting story of life in the United States in the 20th century, with intimate portraits of many of the leaders in all walks of life. The chapters about his uncle, Sigmund Freud, with many hitherto unpublished letters is a well told story which stands on its own. His experiences with the publishing business give an inside view of the development and oddities of this industry. His work with the Waldorf-Astoria, including the famous episode with Oscar of the Waldorf, produces several memorable vignettes.

It is impossible in a review to do more than convey something of the flavor of the book. To begin to list the people and organizations with which he worked until 1961 would be impossible and meaningless. (A list in the back of the book headed "Among Our Clients" contains hundreds of names of organizations and individuals.) And lest we have given the impression that Bernays is always the hero of the book, let us say that he has a disarming way of confessing to numerous mistakes of opinion and judgment which lends creditability. He admits, for example, to turning down ground floor opportunities with Time because he didn't think a news magazine would be successful. His experience with NBC was a frustrating one which he describes with candor, as was his special assignment on behalf of India from which he finally withdrew.

Bernays has a sharp eye for description and knows how to tell a story. His work for Cartier tells about a fascinating merchant with far-ranging influence. He has some good material about the incredible George Washington Hill of Lucky Strike and, in addition, this episode is a good case on how public relations works for a client in supporting his advertising. The Edison Golden Jubilee story is not only a case history on anniversary celebrations, but revealing of the character of Henry Ford. He was in proxy fights, too—the struggle for the control of the American Aviation Corporation—and years before medicare he was in the battle for improved medical service. He makes his twenty years with United Fruit a first-rate business history. And he has a wry chapter about the public relations of the 1939 World's Fair which he claims were completely unsatisfactory and that the recent Fair simply duplicated the mistakes.

Counselors will appreciate his discussion of fees, his staff and his client relationships. He confesses of one long-time client "I do not remember why our Cheney relationship ended ... Professional relationships, I had learned, are not enduring in an impermanent world ... A new policy-maker in the firm, a change in the economic climate, a wave of cutting expenses—any of these can end what appears to be a permanent and fruitful relationship." We can perhaps take comfort in learning that upon many occasions the articulate Bernays confesses to a complete inability to convey public relations to a client and is frustrated thereby. We can sense other frustrations when he writes, "Experts are effective in evaluating the past, but I would rather have poets evaluate the future." We can sympathize with him when he acquires CBS as an account, and puts one of his staff members on the CBS payroll only to have him cancel the Bernays organization at contract renewal time.

It is clear throughout that Bernays has always approached public relations counseling as the product of an individual, rather than of a large impersonally named organization. Thus he used every technique possible for personal promotion, including a periodical publication and involving himself in every kind of movement where he would get additional exposure.

And since his is the cult of the individual, there is bound to be no reference to PRSA or other professional organizations. Neither does he mention many contemporary practitioners. We learn nothing of what he thought of Carl Byoir or Ivy Lee, two counselors he does mention, only that he evidently knew them. And friends of certain other practitioners he mentions will be bound to be upset by his unfriendly characterizations.

Yet, from the overall good of the public relations field, this book does a service in telling the public that the history of this country since World War I is not complete without mentioning the role of public relations, and its beneficial service in the public interest.

No review would be complete without mention of Doris Fleishman Bernays, his wife and associate in his firm. While she chose the role of working primarily behind the scenes, she exerted her own personality as an individual many times, and her efforts to establish her right to use her own name after marriage broke through the existing laws and mores. Her resulting interest in the rights of women sparked action and she has managed a successful career of wife, mother and professional.

Biography of an Idea should be required reading for every practitioner and student of public relations, and it ought to be highly informative and entertaining for those inside and outside the field who are interested in the life and people of the 20th century. To those among us who still might have their doubts, we simply suggest that they read first and then, if they choose, tell us how they would amend the record.

Winter 1966

ELB walking in his garden at 7 Lowell Street in Cambridge, to which he moved from New York in the early sixties to complete his memoirs, *Biography of an Idea*, published by Simon and Schuster in 1965.

The Outlook for Public Relations

Public relations and public relations counsel are here to stay for as long as our democratic society stays. Under the extremes of right or left, Fascism or Communism, there is no room for public relations. Monolithic propaganda supported by censorship, threat and intimidation enforces its ideology on the society. But if our society continues mobile and fluid, competition of ideas and things in the marketplace will continue. Public relations will grow, an increasingly important function. The practitioner will reap benefits in increased rewards in status and other values.

Public relations counsel will be called upon more and more to advise top management in profit and non-profit enterprises on how to adjust in attitude and action to the more complex society on which they depend. Speeded up transportation and communications have already made one room of the three million square miles of this country. A societal technician who effectively advises on the interrelationship of groups and groups and groups and individuals is essential. Anticipating and interpreting public desires and wants to management demands a highly specialized field of competence, often different from that needed to carry on other functions of management.

Forty-three years ago in *Crystallizing Public Opinion,* published in 1923, before the advent of many changes we take for granted today, I defined the scope and functions of modern public relations and public relations counsel. My general thesis was accepted and became a basis for the proliferation of present-day public relations. But after four decades uncertainty appears to prevail as to the direction the profession, so carefully plotted at the time, should take. Some envisage the activity as an information function, applying the arts of communication to inform their publics about an organization. Others, including myself, maintain the function should continue into the future as originally defined—an adviser's service to top-level management on how it should behave, how it should act to win public favor. The life of all institutions in our society depends on public goodwill.

Unfortunately no body like the French Academy exists in this country to preserve the meaning of words. Words are fragile as lace; anyone can set about to modify and distort them.

Definition of Terms

It might be well to define our terms. I have done this before and have done it again in my recently published memoirs *Biography Of An Idea.* But with any new idea, emphasis by repetition is not unimportant. Public relations means exactly what it says, relations of an organization, individual, idea, whatever, with the publics on which it is dependent for its existence. The public relations counsel is the practitioner, a professional, equipped by education, training and experience to give counsel to client or employer on relations with the publics on which the subject depends. He sets about his task by analyzing the relations of the subject and the publics on which it depends, for its social goals. He finds out the adjustments and maladjustments between the subject and these publics. He then advises on the attitudes and actions necessary to attain the social goals, and then interprets the subject to the public. Public relations counsel functions on a two-way street. He interprets public to client and client to public.

I use the words "social goals" advisedly. By definition, a profession is an art applied to a science, in which the primary consideration is public interest, not pecuniary motivation. By this criterion doctors, lawyers, architects are professional men. Other criteria of a profession are educational facilities, a literature, voluntary associations of its members and validation by the state.

Public relations is a profession. It has educational facilities that provide training for practitioners. Three hundred schools of higher learning give courses in public relations. An extensive literature provides an intellectual background for the profession. Three bibliographies published by the University of Minnesota Press, the University of Princeton Press, and the University of Wisconsin Press demonstrate the wide variety of books in the field. It has voluntary associations of members, for general and specialized practitioners.

Hence I disagree with those who say that we are not a profession, that we are a business function, a craft, an art. Public relations is not a business function, because it covers a much wider field of activity. It is not a craft by dictionary definition of what a craft is. When practiced as it should be it is an art applied to a science—not an art.

But the profession today lacks one important element of a profession, validation by the state. The history of professions indicates the need for such validation of public relations. Professions are given higher status by the society because they serve the public interest. Society in turn safeguards itself against malfeasance or malpractice, by licensing the practitioner. This accreditation assures that his capability and character serve the public interest and his profession alike. Talk of accreditation by a voluntary society is meaningless to the broad public and the profession. Without meaningful sanctions for misbehavior, accreditation has little significance. A decent practitioner does not need a code. An indecent one will do lip service to codes and accreditation. Strong sanctions by the state are meaningful. No lawyer wants to be disbarred from practice for malfeasance. No doctor wants to be penalized by withdrawal of his license. I once made a study of codes of different vocations. Each affirmed the justice and equity of certain practices in the field it defined. Each practice so defined was more honored in the breach than in its observance. Lip worship was substituted for reality.

Public relations in the future will include within it all the relations of an organization with its publics. Advertising covers one field of the relations of an organization with its publics. Public relations covers all of them.

Public Relations Counsel of the Future

The public relations counsel of the future will be a generalist and a specialist. No doctor can cover the field of medicine. No lawyer can know all there is to know about every type of law. A public relations counsel of the future will specialize. But he must be a generalist as well. Specialization should never develop to the point where the specialist does not see the woods for the tree. Specialized fields in public relations have already arisen in such areas as civil rights, finance, international relations, health, education, welfare, government, community, corporations, union and union management, arts, media, trade and professional associations, in proxy fights, pricing and legislation. Some general practitioners will remain but there will be fewer of them.

With a greater reservoir of knowledge of what he should do and how to do it and with the increasing complexity of society, the practitioner will need to be a very wise man to be able to analyze and synthesize the tangible and intangible elements that enter into his advice. No computer machine can substitute for judgement based on knowledge and experience.

Outside counsel on public relations will have a place in public relations, as it does in law and medicine. Unhampered independent judgement based on the broadest experience will always be valuable. In our bureaucratic structures, the voice of the individual who has a stable position on the totem pole will not be listened to with the same authority as an independent voice from the outside. And this is especially true if the outside voice earns more money than his opposite number in the internal organization.

What education should practitioners receive? No consensus agrees upon the requisite education. It is time public relations practitioners gave direction to this vital area, for the sake of society and the profession. Institutions of higher learning are constitutionally standoffish to new disciplines. A cultural time lag exists in such institutions' attitudes to public relations. In some instances schools of journalism have assumed taking on the field. This emphasizes informational, not policy, functions of public relations. In others, education is carried on in schools of business administration, oriented towards commerce and industry. The emphasis in education should be in orienting the future practitioner to an understanding of the society as a whole, rather than to one segment of it.

Public Relations Education

The education of the public relations careerist of the future must be along the broadest lines. It must be an education to enable him to cope intelligently with the problems of adjustment in a democratic society. Educational training of the future practitioner should try to make him a man of breadth and understanding, so that he can understand the complicated world we live in rather than to make him a craftsman or technician. Such skills if need be can come later, from experience in the workaday world.

A B.A. degree with honors and emphasis on the humanities and the social sciences from a good university seems to me a good prerequisite for a successful career, with graduate courses in communications and public opinion, to be followed by a working internship.

The effectiveness of the public relations man in the future will depend in part on his education and training. But it will also depend on the comprehension by top management of its obligations to society. Public relations can only be as effective as top management's understanding and willingness to accept and apply advice. In our society, the person who is advised, in the last analysis, decides what is done, not the adviser. The adviser may know more about what is good for the organization than the management, but to be effective the advice must be taken. Maybe the public relations profession has an obligation to educate businessmen and others on what their public responsibilities are.

The future will demand not only top brains in the practitioner but the highest ethics as well, if the profession makes progress. In 1923 I defined the ethics of the practitioner and his obligations to society, client, media and to himself. That holds today as it will tomorrow. We should know clearly what we are talking about when we talk about ethics. We cannot permit, in the future, one code of ethics for the individual in his business or professional life, and another for his private life.

Ethical Obligations

There can be no equivocation as to what the ethical obligations of the public relations man are. I find obfuscating rather than clarifying such statements as those of a public relations leader who said "Nothing has occurred to change my view that business executives sincerely desire to do the right thing as they see it, and are increasingly becoming more public relations minded."

The right thing as the businessman sees it is not necessarily the right thing as the public interest sees it. It may be the wrong thing, as the ethical leader, the consumer, the government or the courts see it. It seems to me the code of conduct for the public relations man is not "rightness" as the businessman sees it, but the rightness as the public interest in its broadest sense demands it.

Another practitioner in the *Public Relations Quarterly* recently indicated that businessmen have an awareness of what the public interest demands. If all businessmen did, business would occupy higher status than it does. And there would be no need for the Consumers Union, the Federal Trade Commission, Better Business Bureaus, drug administrations, and the like. This arrogation that any one group of the society is perfect is unrealistic, to say the least. All members of all groups of our society need continuing elucidation and education on what their public responsibilities are.

Good public relations advice should anticipate the future. The public relations man cannot be a prophet. The lawyer analyzes the past to find a precedent on which he bases his action; a good public relations man anticipates the future in his recommendations. This is no gift of clairvoyance, but rather his ability to evaluate the past and present and project possible future trends. The public relations adviser interprets change to his client so he can anticipate the future in attitude and action.

Research in the social sciences will produce many new findings that will benefit society and that will make the task of advising an adjustment, information and persuasion stand on ever firmer scientific findings.

The professional voluntary public relations association will of course function in the future. But it should not be an American Medical Association fighting a rear guard action to prevent beneficent social change. It should be a forward-looking organization working to advance its field and the society as a whole, and picking areas of broad and progressive public interest.

Fighting for a Better Society
There are many public issues in which the joint intelligence and experience of trained public relations men can play a vital role.

Who is going to fight to make this a better society, if it isn't the public relations men who know presumably how to enlist public opinion? And what about becoming a pressure group to help correct some of the injustices and inequalities of the society? This is the kind of advice we give our clients. Why not practice some of it on ourselves?

Winter 1966

ELB at one of his many out-of-town speaking engagements. He remains healthy enough in his nineties to continue touring the United States regularly, attending public relations meetings and addressing university groups.

Public Relations Council: A Response

*(In the Spring 1975 issue, Neil A. Lavick proposed the establish-
ment of "Public Relations Councils" as an alternative to licensing.
Following is a response.)*

One truth learned in a long lifetime is this: never tackle a
problem as if it were unique, completely standing by itself, unrelated to anything that has happened before. Everything is part of a
whole. Always I try to find what light past-related concepts or
situations can shed on the present. How were such past situations
solved or resolved?

Most problems that face society, a group or individual today
necessarily are related to past experience. Lessons from the past
may be applied to bring about present day solutions.

Finding the right solution to ensure the status of public relations
as a profession cannot be treated as if it were an isolated present day
crisis unrelated to what occurred before. It should be examined and
then treated from the standpoint of how recognized professions of
today, medicine and law for instance, developed and adjusted to
the needs of society, of which they are now so integral a part, and to
their own needs.

This is an entirely different approach from that suggested in the article in the Spring 1975 PRQ advocating Public Relations Councils. Temporizing, piecemeal proposals without clout satisfy neither the needs of the profession nor society. No legal sanctions, for instance, to ensure ethical behavior are attached to the suggested approach. No consideration is given to the history of professions over the last hundreds of years, that have proven what can be done to validate professions in their interest and the public interest. The recent deflation of public relations by Nixon's advisers, wrongly called public relations men, can be effectively met if we take our cue from how other vocations professionalized themselves and follow their example. The development of other professions can serve as a guideline for the public relations profession.

Professions have been under discussion for a long time. Francis Bacon's comment on professions might serve as a stimulus to those of us in public relations who want to see their lifework receive due recognition from society. He said "I hold every man a debtor to his profession, from that which as men do of course seek to receive countenance and profit, so ought they of duty to endeavor themselves, by way of amends, to be a help and an ornament thereunto." Since 1919, my wife and I have attempted to apply this Baconian maxim. In *Crystallizing Public Opinion,* I tried to define the new profession and made a plea for its recognition. In the period of the New Deal, a New York assemblyman, at our suggestion, drew up and introduced a bill in the legislature that asked for licensure of counsel of public relations, based on examination of education, experience and character. Little came of it. But the proposal is even more relevant today than it was then.

Society, through the development of technology and invention, has become increasingly complex over the last centuries and the last decades. Efficiency demands that specialists and experts are provided to keep the many entities in society adjusted and moving along. Organizations of all kinds, profit and non-profit and individuals, as well, need a societal technician, a specialist, the counsel on public relations, who can help them reach their goals, by interpreting the public to them and in turn aiding them to interpret themselves to their publics. This work demands special education, training, experience, high ethical standards that can apply the findings of the social sciences to the problems at issue. A new profession arose to satisfy this need. It was a logical outgrowth from the vocation of press agent and publicity man, a post-World War I development, inspired by Woodrow Wilson's U.S. Committee on Public Information activities to make the world safe for democracy.

All professions have evolved. None has sprung full-grown from the head of any Zeus. England after the Reformation, with the freeing of activities of man from the early church, saw the rise of new professions. The church had dominated the medieval world but not all professions. Physicians and surgeons were organized in guilds. The College of Physicians was founded in 1518, the Company of Barber Surgeons in 1540. In 1745 the Surgeons separated from the Barber Surgeons. The lawyers organized in the eighteenth century. But it was not until the nineteenth century that requirements for licensure by the state developed. Specialization brought with it in England and then in the United States proliferation of educational courses to meet the new demands.

In the United States licensing of professions is nationwide. The important sanction, withdrawal of the license by the state if there be infringement in conduct by the practitioner, is a safeguard society has set up to maintain the integrity of professions.

Public relations by every criterion except one—recognition of status by the state—is a profession. It meets the classical definition of a profession, "a vocation, in which a professed knowledge of some department of learning or science is used in its application to the affairs of others or in the practice of an art founded on it." Or that of the Dictionary of Sociology which says that a profession is a vocation in which an art is applied to a science, and in which the public interest and not pecuniary rewards are the primary consideration.

Public relations has all the attributes of a profession. Here they are: It has a body of knowledge or art. Public relations has an educational process. Since the first course in public relations given by me in 1923 at New York University, 303 institutions of higher learning in 1970 gave 342 teaching programs. Degrees in public relations were given at 89 of them.

Public relations has defined standards of professional qualifications. These may be found in most standard textbooks on public relations or in some of the publications of the Public Relations Society of America. These could serve as a basis for state examinations.

Public relations has standards of conduct already defined in the present codes of the Public Relations Society of America, which could be used as a basis for state adaptation.

As for recognition of status, many professional public relations men and women have already received recognition in the honors bestowed on them. State recognition would enhance such recognition and put public relations on a parity with other professions.

If we want public relations to gain public understanding, recognition and the support it deserves we can follow precedents of law and medicine. We can demand licensure.

The state, through a board of examiners, chosen from the profession, sets up relevant examinations as to character, training and education and experience. Those who pass are permitted to use the title. Should they transgress, the title is withdrawn.

The sanction of bestowal or withdrawal of the title by the state, as in the case of disbarred lawyers, carries with it economic sanctions that give it the clout it needs. As in the case of other vocations newly under licensure, present practitioners can retain their present title until their death. But new practitioners follow the new procedures of licensure after examination.

As to the maintenance of constitutional freedoms under licensure, this does not add or subtract from freedoms. Licensure simply gives state recognition to the fact that the man who calls himself a counsel on public relations, or lawyer or medical doctor, has passed examinations by the state that permit him to assume that title.

Licensure and certification are sound and practical ways to assure the continuity of the public relations profession, based on the experience of other socially desirable professions.

Summer 1975

ELB addressing meeting at the University of Florida upon the occasion of its 50th year of teaching public relations.

Hucksterism
vs.
Public Relations

Some fifty years ago, we recognized society's need for a professional who could advise on a two-way basis, interpreting principal to public and public to principal. Resolutions in communication, transportation and technology had strengthened people power. A vocation developed that enabled all organizations better to meet their social goals, based on action—adjustment to the public, persuasion of and information to the public. Counsels on public relations filled an important social function.

Now come announcements of lecture and seminar series on public relations from the prestigious American Management Association, New York University and the Public Relations Society of America, and *Advertising Age*—announcements which give the false impression that public relations has reverted to a non-professional status and is only a mechanical function of disseminating information, true or false, social or anti-social.

This definition of public relations is a perversion of the original meaning and definition of the profession, validated for over fifty years. But word meanings are as fragile as lace. If public relations is to survive as a profession, as an art applied to a science (social science in this case), immediate action should be taken by professional societies of the vocation to ensure that the identification and integrity of the profession be protected. The way to survive is by state sanctions. That means state registration and licensing which defines the vocation and sets up qualifications in education and experience necessary to practice it.

Giving information to the public is a recognized adjunct of public relations work. But sound action must precede it. Deeds must come before words. Advice on action is the important function of the professional, based on knowledge of the social sciences, individual and group behavior, appraisal of the public's hopes and needs, on social responsibility and on experience in coping with these problems in a professional way.

The American Management Association's announcement cover blazons forth "Make your new PR people work like crazy for one week...So training them won't drive *you* crazy." It lists "skills-building" courses on "the media today" and their definition, "the press release and the press kit," "public relations writing," "the press conference and press interview," "the role of photography in public relations" and "product publicity." These are all part of the skills of public relations.

Not a word about social responsibility, ethics, or the principles of adjustment or persuasion. And public opinion and its measurement are completely ignored.

Comparable omissions occur in the announcement of a One Day High Intensity Course by *Advertising Age* on Publicity & Public Relations. It covers "closing the advertising gap—achieving total market penetration via a coordinated combination of PR and advertising...the public relations equation (exposure = awareness = sales)...how to get editors to publish your publicity pictures," etc. Not a word about underlying principles that govern advice to bring about adjustment or understanding.

The so-called Public Relations Management Seminars of New York University, sponsored by the University and, shockingly enough, the Public Relations Society of America, do no better. Much on the mechanics; nothing about ethics, social responsibility, or the broad principles on which professional public relations are based.

It is high time to define public relations with state sanctions to ensure that hucksterism does not replace professionalism.

Fall 1976

ELB on the front porch of his home in Cambridge, Massachusetts, winter 1985, with hat from Poland given to him by his son-in-law, Dr. Richard Held, head of the MIT psychology department, after a visit to that country.

Needed:
An Ombudsman for
Public Relations

Americans must not lose confidence in freedoms guaranteed by our Constitution because of abuses stemming from these very freedoms.

I shall discuss abuses in the area of freedom of expression in print media, action to curb them and make recommendations to the public relations and other professions to safeguard public and members of the profession alike.

The December fifteenth *Variety* quotes Walter Cronkite charging that a page one story in the *Enquirer* stated he believes in flying saucers. Mr. Cronkite said this was a total lie and that the writer had not interviewed him, as stated.

American society has begun to protect itself against such abuses in the organization of the National News Council, a privately funded body that investigates complaints of inaccuracy or unfairness in the news media, print and broadcast. Findings of fault or exoneration are released after investigation. Standards for truth in media are promoted by such action.

Use of ombudsmen by some newspapers—e.g., the *Boston*

Globe—is another method. Complaints are investigated; findings published.

Some newspapers like *The New York Times* have corrections columns. Unfortunately all errors are not corrected. Some have letter columns with corrections.

Unfortunately book publishing has no such instrumentalities. Thousands of books are published annually by publishers varying in integrity from high to low, very low. Many so-called non-fiction volumes contain lies, inaccuracies, false conclusions based on ignorance, bias or malice.

False statements about reputable individuals or organizations in books damage reputations. Victims of such character assassination have little redress. A book is published and distributed, often with no second edition. Some conscienceless publishers and authors make no corrections. They have little to fear from law. The victim can only complain. The false accusation stands on the victim's record. Bibliographers and others accept the printed lie at face value.

Today a lazy, ignorant or malicious non-fiction writer can blacken reputations with impunity under the guise of writing history.

Libel suits may be instituted against author and/or publisher by victims of this freedom to lie. But under American law, libel suits have to prove intent to defame the victim, almost impossible to prove. Even if libel laws were less stringent, militating factors against instituting suits prevail. A libel suit, reported in media, spreads false accusations to people who may be ignorant of them. Most books do not have large sales and most people would not hear of the false attack. A law suit often defeats its purpose. High costs for legal outlay preclude a law suit for most victims of lies.

One other danger from present abuse. Book reviewers, even of the most respectable media, often do not have thorough knowledge of facts in the book reviewed. They accept the author's word as truth, when it is fantasy. Their reviews pass on falsities of the author, sometimes reflecting on an individual's integrity. Readers accept the reviewer because they trust his medium.

Here are some ways to supplement the National News Council and newspaper ombudsmen.

I suggest the Public Relations Society of America assume leadership and appoint an ombudsman. Public relations professionals are often the victims of unjustified character assassination. On complaint, the Society would weigh such accusations against members. A report of findings would be published.

I recommend other professional organizations in the United States adopt ombudsmen functions for members falsely attacked in media.

These steps will not cure liars. But they will establish for the record the veracity or untruth of stories, which go uncorrected today and do damage to the reputation of honorable men and women.

Winter 1976

ELB congratulating Carol A. Wolicki on her having completed a nationwide telephone linkup with other public relations executives, 1985.

Down With Image, Up With Reality

Everybody knows—or should know—that communication is a two way process. Conveying depends not only on what we say but also on whether the individual to whom we send the message understands our intended meaning from our words.

Correct choice of words to express meaning takes some understanding of semantics.

This is particularly true in discussing new fields of action—public relations as an instance. We must use words that accurately define meaning. No French Academy in this country ensures purity of the language.

During the last years, some public relations practitioners have used the word "image" in connection with their profession. They use the terms like "image problems" and "image making." Only recently a high executive of the Public Relations Society of America at New York headquarters was quoted in the *Wall Street Journal* as referring to the public relations profession's carrying on, among other activities, "consultation with company managements on general image problems."

As for me, the word "image" in association with public relations is and has been on my "index expurgatorius" and will remain so.

There is good reason for this. *The Random House Dictionary of the English Language* gives 13 definitions for the noun "image." None refers to a professional public relations practitioner's primary activity—being obsessed with the importance of reality. The practitioner deals with attitude and/or action change of his principal, to meet social objectives.

Here is the *Random House Dictionary*'s definition of the noun, "image."

1. A physical likeness or representation of a person, animal or thing, photographed, painted, sculptured or otherwise made visible.
2. An optical counterpart or appearance of an object, such as is produced by reflection from a mirror, refraction by a lens, or the passage of luminous rays through a small aperture and their reception on a surface.
3. A mental representation; idea; conception.
4. Psychol. A mental representation of something previously perceived, in the absence of the original stimulus.
5. Form; appearance; semblance: God created man in his own image.
6. Counterpart; copy: That child is the image of his mother.
7. A symbol; emblem.
8. A type; embodiment: Red-faced, he was the image of frustration and consternation.
9. A description of something in speech or writing: Casually, almost effortlessly, he created some of the most beautiful images in the language.
10. An idol: They knelt down before graven images.
11. Rhet. A figure of speech, especially a metaphor or a simile: With adroit turns of phrase the author created images as vivid as their presence itself.
12. Math. The point or set of points in the range corresponding to a designated point in the domain of a given function.
13. Archaic. An illusion or apparition.

To use a fuzzy, indeterminate word like "image" to define hard reality is not communicating the true meaning of public relations.

The interest of both public and profession demands that the word "image" referring to public relations be eliminated. Practitioners should cease use of the word to describe their activities. The word "image" makes the reader or listener believe public relations deals with shadows and illusions. This word belittles a profession dealing with hard facts of behavior, attitudes and actions, that requires ability to evaluate public opinion and advise clients or employers on how to adjust to gain socially acceptable goals and to inform and persuade the public.

We must describe our activities with meaningful words, comprehensible to all who determine the climate of opinion in a democratic society.

Spring 1977

Mr. and Mrs. Gary Quackenbush with ELB overlooking San Francisco. Quackenbush is a public relations practitioner in the Bay Area.

Four Steps Towards Enhancing the Future of Public Relations

In World War I, as a staff member of the U.S. Committee on Public Information, I helped disseminate Woodrow Wilson's words, "the war to end war," "make the world safe for democracy," "the Fourteen Points." This intensified American and Allied morale, won over neutrals and weakened enemy morale. Observers said "words won the war."

Returning from the Paris Peace Conference, I applied my wartime experience to peacetime pursuits. I named my new calling "publicity direction." My prewar activity had been publicity for Caruso, the Russian Ballet, Metropolitan Opera, and Broadway stars.

Soon I learned that directing clients' activities to secure public visibility was inconclusive. They might profit, but another action of theirs, impinging on the public, might deflate the newly won goodwill.

My partner and wife, Doris E. Fleischman Bernays, and I decided to rename and reorient our activity. We decided clients must be advised on all actions, after research and interpretation of their publics. Then counsel them on informing and persuading publics to accept the product, service or idea.

This was no one-way street of publicity, press agentry, flackery. We called this two-way street activity counsel on public relations. I wrote *Crystallizing Public Opinion,* the first book on the subject, and gave the first public relations course at New York University, to further this concept.

This was an idea whose time had come. Public relations flourished throughout society, over the free world, wherever competition of ideas, services and products prevailed. Universities initiated public relations courses. Practitioners multiplied. The Public Relations Society of America and specialized associations arose. Literature grew to 15,000 entries.

The profession kept pace with an increasingly complex society, the result of communication, transportation, technology revolutions, people's expanded expectations, and people power. Society needed applied social science professionals to advise on adjustment, information and persuasion.

And then—exact time and place unknown—public relations became for many practitioners, employers, clients a synonym for communicating. *Fortune* in 1949 wrote that the main reason business wasn't rolling in goodwill was that about 95% of the activity labelled public relations was sheer press agentry. Recently some practitioners have even changed their titles to communications directors and the like. This ignores World War I historians' pronouncement that "words won the war and lost the peace" and the truth that actions speak louder than words.

The profession's and the public's interest demands activity now to assure the real public relations' future.

1. The Public Relations Society of America should demand state registration and licensing to establish standards of competence and ethics. Today everyone can call themselves public relations practitioners.

2. Public relations associations should demand curriculum changes in public relations teaching at universities and colleges. Communications and journalism colleges, where public relations is mainly taught, treat it as an appendage, emphasizing writing skills, not social science.

3. The Public Relations Society of America in its own courses should emphasize social science, instead of writing skills.

4. The public relations profession should educate potential clients and employers to public relations' true definition and value. A study of executive help wanted advertisements in the Sunday *New York Times* and the *Wall Street Journal* reveals abysmal ignorance of public relations, now equated with press agentry and publicity.

This demands change. A half century of progress in professional practice should be maintained. The free world needs societal professionals in adjustment, information and persuasion.

Summer 1977

Manuel Viscasillas (left), head of Latino department at Campbell Ewald advertising agency in Miami, and the Honorable Francis Duehev, Mayor of Cambridge, Mass., with ELB at his 94th birthday party, 1985.

In Praise of Books

This column is in praise of books and their importance in the professional practice of public relations. All research shows Americans do not place the value on books they should. Library usage and the book publishing industry confirm these findings. Our own counseling experience over fifty years in varied fields indicates books are a last, rather than first, resort in most problem solving and policy setting. Top executives of *Fortune's* 500 corporations have told me they have no time to read books. Nor do they have them tapped for wisdom, understanding and facts.

Books have played an important role in establishing the validity of our profession and in our counsel to clients, enabling us to cope with new problems as we met them.

As early as 1920, I consistently read *Publishers Weekly* and the *Library Journal,* bibles in their respective fields. They kept us and still keep us abreast in their reviews of new books related to our field and those of our clients or prospective clients, months before the books appear in book stores or are reviewed in the popular press, if they are reviewed. These books provide new insights and information. We often knew more about the problem of our clients than the chief executive officer we dealt with. He often thought he was so busy that he had no time to read books.

Even before scientific market research and opinion polling,

reading the right new book by a wise author made it unnecessary to apply hunch and insight. We could base advice on more than these so often unverified tools of public relations practitioners. Freelance outside readers brought us abstracts of x numbers of books on insurance, for example, the morning after we had signed a contract with the insurance company. And we could discuss problems with its officers intelligently.

Early in our work, we established a public relations library in our office, with books on psychology, social psychology, cultural anthropology, sociology, economics, management, semantics, linguistics. It included also many directories, yearbooks, almanacs, and other compendia important for the secondary aspect of our activity, for information useful in persuasion and communication to publics, after client attitudes and actions had been modified.

A most important category of books in our library were and are bibliographies covering the most varied fields, including public relations. These books refer to volumes in the fields they cover, often with abstracts to aid the researcher.

Our contact with practitioners over the years indicates that many practitioners are unaware of these bibliographies, so helpful in assuring they do not have to be Columbuses and Magellans with the problem at hand. They can start where others left off. Here are a few such volumes, old and new:

Harwood L. Childs. *A Reference Guide to the Study of Public Opinion.* Princeton: Princeton University Press, 1934, with a preface by Edward L. Bernays.

Harold D. Lasswell et al. *Propaganda and Promotional Activities.* Minneapolis: The University of Minnesota Press, 1935.

Public Relations: Edward L. Bernays and the American Scene, A Bibliography. Westwood, Mass.: F. W. Faxon Co., 1951.

Scott Cutlip. *A Public Relations Bibliography.* 2nd ed. Madison: The University of Wisconsin Press, 1965. (Covers through 1963)

Robert L. Bishop. *Public Relations: A Comprehensive Bibliography.* Ann Arbor: The University of Michigan Press, 1974. (Covers 1964 through 1972)

Robert L. Bishop has also compiled supplements to this last book, for 1973-4, and 1975. These were published by *Public Relations Review.*

It is permissible, I think, to add that F. W. Faxon will publish early in 1978 an updated version of the third item in this list, *Public Relations: Edward L. Bernays and the American Scene, A Bibliography,* compiled by Keith A. Larson, with 4079 items listing writings by and about the Bernays in books and periodicals, 1905-1977.

Fall 1977

ELB with Tim Colwell, public relations manager of Parker Drilling Company, Tulsa, Oklahoma, and later president of the PRSA Tulsa chapter, which invited Bernays as its guest in 1985.

A Deplorable
Cultural Time Lag

"Creative skills publicity generation"
"Excellent business writing skill and contacts"
"Developing press relations releases"
"Outstanding writer"
"Experienced creative writer"
"Directing all press relations activities"
"Seek an accomplished science writer"
"Proven capabilities in press relations"

No, these are not excerpts from advertisements seeking a press agent, publicity man or woman. These are verbatim lines from recent large help-wanted advertisements in the New York Sunday *Times* and the *Wall Street Journal,* headlined Public Relations Pro, Director Public Relations, Public Relations Coordinator, Public Relations. These advertisements, inserted mostly by large corporations, some from nonprofit organizations, were all seeking executives for their so called public relations functions. Yet not one of these advertisements specified the qualifications essential in the public relations function—knowledge and understanding of human relationships, how to measure and appraise public attitudes, how to bring about adjustment between the public interest and the private interest of the principal. Not a word about the essential knowledge of the social sciences the applicant should possess, a knowledge basic to giving sound advice on group relationships between the advertiser and the publics on which the advertiser is dependent.

These advertisements all displayed a colossal ignorance of the profession of public relations and its function of counseling the principals on how to conduct themselves in our society to achieve their social goals. The advertisements demonstrate a deplorable cultural time lag in the understanding by the policy and decision makers of large corporations and other institutions, of the profession and what it can do for them in meeting their social objectives.

These advertisements might all have been published in the pre-World War I period, when "the public be damned" was the dominant rule and white washing by words was the order of the day. Words were thought to speak louder than actions. They, rather than acts, were then the tools of attempted adjustment.

Today's situation demands correction. It deprives organizations, profit and nonprofit, because of ignorance of professional services by individuals, who could use them to adjust to society. It deprives professionals of opportunities to serve the public interest, coincidental with their private interests.

This is the logical area for the Public Relations Society of America and the other professional associations in public relations to get busy and bring potential employers and clients up to date on what the profession is and does. Time and effort spent on such activities instead of promoting teaching seminars on writing skills would better serve the public and the profession.

Public relations practitioners are not flacks, press agents. They are societal technicians who advise their clients or employers on what attitudes and actions to take that will enable them more effectively to reach their social goals. They are practitioners who analyze the adjustments or maladjustments between a principal and the publics on whom principal is dependent. They advise and counsel on attitude and action to meet goals. Only after this, do they perform and persuade publics concerned.

Here is a task through which the PRSA and other public relations groups can take leadership in a society which needs the advice public relations practitioners can provide to make a better adjusted world.

Winter 1977

Chet Burger of Chester Burger & Company, New York, and ELB

Defining
Public Relations

In the 1920's, a new profession, counsel on public relations, was conceived and founded to meet the needs of an increasingly complex society for adjustment. The new professional advised principals on adjustment of attitudes and action with the publics on whom viability depended. As the lawyer advised on legal relations, the public relations counsel advised on relations with the public. The profession's principles, practices and ethics were laid down in my book *Crystallizing Public Opinion,* published in 1923.

Counsel on action was based on applied social science. Information to and persuasion of the public to support services, products or ideas of the principal, after action was taken, was an ancillary activity. Actions speak louder than words. Action precedes words. That year, I gave the first public relations course at an institution of higher learning, New York University, *Public Relations, A Course on Theory and Practical Method.* Emphasis was on study of public opinion, how it functioned and how to adjust to it. Purpose of the course was to give students understanding of problems of adjustment.

Fourteen years later, in 1937, my partner-wife Doris E. Fleischman and I made a study of U.S. public relations and related courses, published in a pamphlet, "Universities—Pathfinders in Public Opinion." We uncovered widespread growth of related courses—on public opinion, its measurement, on social psychology, collective behavior, theory of psychological movements, social psychology, collective behavior, group behavior, formation of public opinion, also some public relations courses. We omitted courses in journalism, advertising and writing skills in our study.

The same year, in an article in the first issue of *The Public Opinion Quarterly,* I wrote: "The increasing attention given by universities, publicists and writers to the importance of sound public relations . . . made business aware of the need for modifying its attitudes and actions to conform to public demands, as well as for getting the public to understand its position."

In 1937, the United States was emerging from a debilitating depression. Roosevelt's New Deal was reestablishing public confidence. People power was expressing itself. Business needed public relations counsel to reestablish itself with a stronger and more vocal public. Other sectors of the society followed suit.

In the last four decades, the public relations profession and public relations education have spread throughout the free world. And many ethical professional practitioners practice public relations as it was conceived. But of course, the success of these practitioners brought in many individuals, who called themselves public relations practitioners, who had neither the training, education or ethics to practice.

This problem can be met, as it has been in the case of other professions by licensing and registration by the state, after examination; but another problem must also be met: that public relations education be geared to the needs of the society and the survival of the profession.

Three recent studies of public relations education, one worldwide and two in the United States, show a situation that threatens the continuity of the profession. These surveys, the Oeckl study world-wide and the Bateman-Cutlip and Walker studies in the United States, indicate that the meaning of the words "public relations" varies. In the United States, over 75% of public relations courses are in schools or departments of journalism or communication. Public relations is treated generally as an adjunct of communication. Words are the core of study. The major emphasis is on writing skills, not on the social sciences. Graduates of regular and special courses have primarily been taught to be press agents, publicity people, flacks. These are not unimportant in a mass communications world. But these graduates are movers of words. Public relations deals primarily with advice on action, based on social responsibility.

It is high time public relations leadership take action to reverse these conditions in the public interest and that of the profession. The introduction of licensing and registration by the state would of course help solve the educational situation. For if proper qualifications for practice were set by the state, higher education would have to take its orientation from such action.

The new leadership of the Public Relations Society of America and that of the International Public Relations Association has important problems to solve.

Spring 1978

Plan Your Future—
Don't Gamble on It

The United States gambling industry is almost a fifteen-billion-dollar industry, *Business Week* recently pointed out. Millions of Americans would rather gamble on their future than plan for it.

The soundest approach to reach our goals is a planned approach. Defining and working towards specific objectives is an underlying principle of effective public relations. This is true for all profit and nonprofit organizations and individuals.

One of the most difficult problems of public relations practitioners is to get their clients or employers to decide on goals and objectives. Only if practitioners know the goals and objectives of their principals can they, as societal technicians, advise them on the attitudes and actions essential to meet their goals, with their publics. We live in a highly competitive and complex society. Unless goals are clearly defined and strategy and tactics planned to attain them, we become the victims of chance.

In a long lifetime advising clients covering the most varied activities, we have found that many function on a day to day, week to week, month to month, year to year, decade to decade basis without clearly defined goals. Economic units, of course, see profit as a goal, but by itself that is not enough. There are many elements to consider: their goodwill with the publics on which they depend, their place in the market, their growth, etc. Nonprofit units carry on their services without well defined goals. And individuals move from job to job fortuitously.

There are definite principles that govern identification of goals and working towards them. And, incidentally, they apply not only to the client or employer of the public relations practitioner, but also to the practitioners themselves. Unless you know where and when you want to land somewhere and whether you have the potential to get there, you are wasting time and effort. You become victim or beneficiary of chance.

First, decide on the long-time approach. The period may vary. An individual of thirty may plan for a thirty-five year goal. A corporation may plan for ten years, because of uncertainties. A nonprofit organization, like a university, may plan ahead for a longer period. A long-term goal for an individual may indicate what he wants to do, where and when, what he wants to contribute to the society of which he is a part and what he expects to get from the society. It will outline the reactions he expects from the relevant publics for his or her ideas, goods, services. It will define the satisfactions expected from personal life. For a corporation, goals may be set in objective terms, percentage of the market, profit margins and profits, dollar value, number of employees, physical plants and locations and, of course, what attitudes and actions are to be expected from the many publics on which viability depends.

And since we are living in an era of increasing social responsibility, the goals of social responsibility will also be defined.

After our long-term goals have been decided on, the next step is research. Research will determine whether the long-term goals set are realistic or unrealistic. Such public opinion or/and market research may be carried out by well known professionals, the

Gallups, Ropers, Harrises, etc. or if funds are not available, by the unit concerned.

The research will determine whether long-term goals will need to be reoriented because they are unrealistic. Research will also determine what intermediate and immediate goals should be. The immediate term may be a year or so, the intermediate term longer, depending on the time of the long-term goal.

Research will also reveal what strategies to use to reach goals—what actions and attitudes of the unit need to be modified—what themes and appeals should be applied to what publics—in what proportions and by what timing to apply the four M's—mindpower, manpower, mechanics and money—to achieve the goals. And research will also aid in the timing of the tactics to be undertaken with internal and external publics to win the goals.

Research will also reveal whether logical or illogical sequences will best reach the goals. So much emphasis is put on the importance of logic in our educational systems, that we must not forget to prepare for illogical sequences as well as logical ones.

The planning for goals places the planner at a great advantage over the non-planner. Public relations practitioners who adopt this method for their principals as well as for themselves will find life more satisfying all around.

Summer 1978

ELB in his Cambridge office with photographs of some of his clients on the wall.

Education for PR:
A Call to Action

From the vantage point of practicing public relations for over half a century, I consider it high time for those interested in preserving the profession to come to its aid now.

I refer particularly to the need for ensuring the kind of college and university education that will serve as a foundation for the practice of the profession. My close examination of several comprehensive recent surveys of public relations higher education shows that, at the present time, in the United States and throughout the free world, there is a wide gap between what is taught and what should be taught to prepare young people for their public relations careers.

These surveys, and my personal observation of university and college courses and their students, reveal that public relations is treated by and large as a minor adjunct of schools of journalism and communications, when it should be treated as applied social science. It is both encouraging and significant that at a recent international conference of public relations societies in Mexico City, due to the efforts of Frank W. Wylie, president of the Public Relations Society of America, and Sam Black, Secretary General of the International Public Relations Society, a sound definition of public relations was adopted that revolves around the concept of public relations as applied social science.

Present-day activities of higher education for public relations, on the other hand, stress skills in writing and communication. It is sound that public relations societies now realize the importance of stressing the true meaning of public relations.

Revolutions in technology, transportation and communications have made the world increasingly complex. All elements of our society need a professional societal technician to aid in adjusting them to their publics. This cannot be done by emphasis on words by themselves, if it is to have lasting effect. It demands action, action based on social responsibility that will bring about adjustment between publics and the party concerned.

The action must be based on applied social science, applying to the problem at hand what social scientists have learned about group and individual behavior. This cannot be done effectively by hunch and insight. It is done by applying the findings of psychology, social psychology, cultural anthropology, history, economics, etc. to the problems at issue. Communication to publics may or may not follow after such advice has brought action. Actions must precede words. Actions speak louder than words. Understanding of the policies that underlie sound action are the bases of good public relationships.

I have been told by people who should know better that the emphasis being put on writing skills and the use of words in public relations higher education is because young people go into these primary jobs in public relations. That is, of course, poppycock. Medical college students who want to become surgeons are not taught how to wield scalpels and knives before they are taught the basics about the human body, the blood stream, the skeletal structure, the nervous system and much else. To put emphasis on writing skills in public relations is comparable.

One immediate step is to remove accreditation of courses and sequences in public relations from the supervision of the Association for Education in Journalism. From the public's standpoint, having a body with that name accredit public relations courses and sequences is like having the surgical instrument manufacturers association accredit courses in surgery at medical college, or law book publishers associations accrediting law courses. Assuredly communications is an adjunct or ancillary activity in public relations. But the social sciences are its basis. If any outside body is to be concerned, besides the Public Relations Society of America, it might be some group like the Society for the Psychological Study of Social Issues.

The present accrediting body is the American Council on Journalism Education with 23 members, representing 17 varied groups of educators and professionals in journalism and communication. Among them are the National Press Photographers Association, the Radio Television News Directors Association, the Western Newspaper Foundation, the American Newspaper Publishers Association, the American Society of Newspaper Editors, the American Association of Schools and Departments of Journalism, the Association for Education in Journalism, the American Society of Journalism School Administrators—and the Public Relations Society of America.

Not a social science group among them.

Public relations, in its own interest and the public interests, needs a new deal in higher education.

Fall 1978

Translating Meaning
into Action

The important element of a civilized society is language. Language enables people to understand each other. But words have a common meaning to bring about mutual understanding. This is true whatever the boundaries within which the words are used. But even a common language of the group that uses it presents barriers to common understanding of many important elements in our lives. For instance, the true meaning of optometrist, opthalmologist and optician remain fuzzy in the public mind. This also holds for the words public relations and counsel on public relations. In this latter case, even many practitioners do not know the true meaning.

Older professions suffer less from such misunderstanding. The word symbols "medical doctor" and "lawyer" have common meaning in the United States, Zanzibar and the Hebrides.

This common meaning in the professions has come about through law. The state protects the meaning of the words for people and the profession alike.

Public relations, now over half a century old, suffers greatly from misunderstanding of its meaning. First defined in *Crystallizing Public Opinion* in 1923, it has naturally suffered from youth.

But also because it has not been defined by law. This lack of specific meaning prevails in this country and throughout the free world. Even the so-called extracurricular courses sponsored by the Public Relations Society of America appear to confuse public relations with old line press agentry, flackery, publicity. Emphasis is put on writing skills and media, instead of on basic social sciences which would enable practitioners to give advice on conduct in their practice.

A recent comment to me from John H. Wherry, executive director of the prestigious National School Public Relations Association, illustrates my point. Public relations practitioners in public education practice under eleven different titles: directors of communication, directors of public information, directors of school community relations, special project coordinators, special assistants to the superintendent, public affairs directors, publications administrators, administrative assistants, communication editors, information specialists and sometimes directors of public relations.

This sad situation brings about misunderstanding by public and profession alike of just what public relations is and does. If these same individuals were practicing law or medicine this would not be the case. They would be known as lawyers and doctors and would be carrying out a function for which they had been trained, registered and licensed by the state.

A recent happening in Mexico City may spark improvement of the situation. Frank W. Wylie, president of the Public Relations Society of America, and Sam Black, secretary-treasurer of the International Public Relations Association took the initiative. The definition they proposed was adopted by the First World Assembly of Public Relations and First World Forum in Public Relations, held August 11, 1978.

It read: "Public relations practice is the art and social science of analyzing trends, predicting their consequences, counselling organization leaders and implementing planned programs of action which will serve both the organization's and the public interest." This definition follows the one laid down in 1923, since subverted and much misused.

Public relations practitioners and public relations associations everywhere in the free world might well cooperate in carrying out a world wide program to translate this meaning into action.

The quickest way is for them to have the state register and license public relations practitioners after qualifying examination as to education, training and character. Only licensed practitioners who have passed the examinations would be permitted to call themselves public relations counsel. Economic sanctions are applied by the state and the license to practice is withdrawn if the practitioner deviates from the code of conduct. This procedure would define the term public relations for the public and the profession alike. Present so-called accreditation methods without economic sanctions are ludicrous and of little value in bringing about that common meaning and understanding, so basic to the survival and growth of a needed profession.

Winter 1978

Sam Black (left), former president of International Public Relations Society and editor of its magazine and good friend of ELB, with other participants in the University of Florida's 50th anniversary of teaching public relations, 1984, Gainesville, Florida.

What Is Professional Development?

A one-page announcement of the Public Relations Society of America recently arrived in the morning mail. Captioned in large type "The Professional Development Program Preview January to May 1979," it listed the titles, dates and locations of eighteen lectures and workshops.

The caption conveys the meaning that these lectures and workshops cover a professional development program for public relations. Such a program would deal with findings of social scientists about human behavior and human relations, with motives and attitudes, with approaches to adjustment and social responsibility. The program would deal with the meaning of symbols, linguistics and semantics, with discussions of socially responsible action and how reason, persuasion and information may affect public opinion. Basic subjects from the social sciences would be discussed that would lead to greater understanding by practitioner auditors to apply social science to problems of everyday life. Public relations practitioners advise their principals on attitudes and actions to take to bring about leadership and adjustment and they can only do so intelligently if they have this knowledge.

The listings do not bear out the caption. The lectures and

workshops deal mainly with how to become a better flack, press agent, publicity man or woman. The perpetrators of this announcement might well be accused of mislabeling.

Certainly there is room for messengers of words in a mass communications society like ours. Messengers of words serve a useful purpose in our society. They are as important to a public relations practitioner as surgical instruments are to a surgeon. But teaching about surgical instruments should not be confused with the teaching of how to be a surgeon. Surgeons needed to know about the human body and how it functions before they use surgical instruments.

Of eighteen sessions listed in the so-called Professional Development Program Preview, fourteen deal with press agent techniques. They cover writing and editing employee/internal publications, understanding public information techniques, breaking the media barrier, writing workshop, design and graphics workshop, working effectively with broadcasters, executing information programs, government public information, financial communications workshop, successful feature placement, internal/external radio and television, the speech as an effective public relations tool, effective employee internal communications programs. No mention anywhere of the social sciences and how to apply their findings to everyday problems of human relationships.

Over 50 years ago, in 1923, this writer gave at New York University the first course ever given on public relations. These earliest lectures emphasized the study of public opinion, the psychology of individuals and groups and how maladjustments between them are handled. These lectures placed emphasis on how and why people behave as they do, how to intensify favorable attitudes, convert those on the fence and negate negative attitudes and always in the public interest. The public relations practitioner was envisaged as an applied social scientist, along the lines of the recent definition adopted by the Mexico City conference of world-wide public relations organizations.

Of what possible use can these so-called courses and lectures on professional development be if their listeners do not have knowledge of the latest findings on human behavior? How will they know how to use actions and words and picture symbols intelligently and effectively to accomplish socially sound objectives, unless they first understand how and why human beings behave as they do?

These lectures and workshops may produce better press agents. But assuredly public relations professional development lectures and workshops demand imparting different knowledge than this one does.

In an increasingly complex society in which the viability of a principal depends on adjustments to his publics, the public relations practitioner fills an important, much needed function as a societal technician.

Why should a professional association of public relations practitioners so cavalierly treat the profession it represents?

Spring 1979

Denny Griswold, former employee of ELB and now publisher of *Public Relations News*, with ELB at his 94th birthday party in Cambridge, Mass., 1985.

Needed: A New
Master's Degree

W_e all talk about the increasing complexity of our world
and the difficulties of bringing about mutual understanding and
adjustment between the diversified groups and individuals in our
society. We do little about it. Cultural time lag dominates our
society. Adulteration affecting thousands is punishable with a
fine; adultery affecting four people, with a prison term.

This cultural time lag persists in higher education. Harvard
University's John F. Kennedy School of Government, in its latest
catalogue, lists no courses on polling, public opinion or public
relations. The Harvard Graduate School of Business Administration has no course on public relations, although many of the
largest corporations in the United States have vice presidents in
charge of public relations. The cultural time lag persists even in
universities that do teach public relations. For the most part such
teaching is tucked away in schools of journalism and mass communications. There it takes a back seat. Writing skills instruction,
instead of social science, dominates baccalaureate degree courses.
True public relations is stifled by journalism administrators who
mistakenly believe public relations is flackery and propaganda,
dependent on words, graphics and news judgments.

We have been fighting cultural time lag for many years, with little progress, I might add.

But today we submit an idea whose time has come and which may safeguard the usefulness and continuity of public relations, and enhance its prestige.

The idea came to me after I observed the mess all parties concerned—public utilities, the state and national government—made of the Three Mile Island nuclear disaster—a public relations disaster, too. The public was not dealt with as it should have been before, during or after the disaster. Advance polls apparently had not been made to evaluate public understanding of nuclear energy, its nomenclature and its jargon. Many sources of information, national, state and private, instead of one source, gave out information about the disaster and obfuscated the public. Verbiage used was misunderstood and misinterpreted. Public relations practitioners associated with the situation did not act as if they were fully aware of the scientific aspects of nuclear energy. The result was chaos.

Here is the idea. That universities set up graduate courses for a master's degree in public relations and various specialized fields such as science, medicine, law, social service, business administration, chemistry, etc., and give combined degrees to the graduating student, such as Master of Public Relations and Medical Doctor, Master of Public Relations and MBA, Master of Public Relations and LLB. A public relations practitioner in the complex world not only needs to be a professional who can apply the findings of the social sciences to problems of adjustment and human understanding. He also needs expertise in the field he is advising and consulting with.

Carl Stern of the National Broadcasting Co. and Fred Graham of Columbia Broadcasting illustrate my point. They cover legal matters. They are trained journalists and graduate lawyers. Dr. Lawrence K. Altman of the *New York Times* is a graduate physician and covers medical matters as a trained journalist.

There is every reason why large universities with many colleges that now give master's degrees in public relations should act in the public interest, convenience and necessity to carry out such a program in joint master's degrees.

Summer 1979

Dr. Otto Butz, president of Golden State University, San Francisco, with ELB upon the occasion of the university's naming its public relations program after him. Bernays gave a speech inaugurating the program in San Francisco.

Public Relations for Voluntary Social Service Organizations

The United Way and other voluntary social service organizations validate the American principle observed by DeTocqueville over a century ago, that voluntary association is a striking part of the American way of life. It reflects a basic truth, that united we stand, divided we fall.

Underlying principles and practices, in my judgment, should dominate actions of voluntary social service agencies in meeting their goals with the publics on which they depend. Sound actions must precede communications, to be effective. Actions speak louder than words. Historians after World War I wrote that words won the war, but lost the peace.

Public relations officials of voluntary service organizations must function not only as communicators but as advisers to principals on policies and actions that will bring public support. They must function on a two-way street, interpreting publics to the organization and interpreting the organization to the public, after action, consistent with public needs and desires, has been taken.

This conclusion is based on six decades of observation and

experience with voluntary organizations in the social welfare field as board member, volunteer, professional and volunteer consultant on public relations. And, incidentally, as a member of the United Way public relations policy committee in Boston for several years.

Six decades ago hunch and insight were mainsprings of gaining public support for voluntary associations. My first experience in 1920 illustrates this. World War I had interrupted the building program of a large federation of charities, as they were then called, in New York. I suggested invitations to the opening drive dinner be sent out, pasted on one side of a large building brick. On the five additional sides was promotional material about the building program. Postal rates were no deterrent then. No brick recipient could throw the invitation away. It would wreck the waste basket. Instead, the invitation served as a paper weight on the prospect's desk, a continual reminder of the obligation to attend the dinner. An all-night mailing bureau after the dinner multigraphed a thank-you letter to all attendants, referring to a chance happening at the dinner. Mailed at New York's main post office, letters were delivered next morning to the surprise of the recipient. The building drive became a cause célèbre. The buildings were constructed.

But today we live in a different world. Revolutions in technology, transportation and communications have changed our society. People power has accelerated. And all institutions need to respond to the changing patterns of society on a much more scientific basis.

Contemporary academicians and researchers provide knowledge of new communications approaches just as researchers at schools of social welfare provide new action-related approaches to coping with problems of social welfare.

Typical of the new approach to problems is a 69-page pamphlet, "Motivations for Charitable Giving," an excellent reference guide. It contains abstracts of books and periodicals dealing with the sociological, psychological, economic, philosophical and religious bases for giving. The pamphlet is published by an informal association of executives of welfare organizations and their legal advisers at 1 Dupont Circle NW, Washington, D.C.

Now a few words as to the background faced in meeting problems of survival. In the United States, we are a highly competitive society in which competition for the hearts, minds and money goes on relentlessly for both profit and non-profit causes. Through many communications media, adult Americans are exposed to hundreds of messages daily to affect their attitudes and actions. Welfare organizations compete for attention and action of this public, whose consciousness is massaged by experts and amateurs for all manner of activities.

These appeals have brought about in the voluntary sector of social welfare, according to The American Association of Fund-raising Council in 1978, 38.1 billion dollars for varied voluntary activities in the United States.

Members of the highly regarded United Way will find this connection helps in financial support from the public. But, at the same time, they must also win support of the public on the basis of their own identities. They must know how to capitalize on relationship with the United Way and how to cope with the problem of winning the public's support.

Here are some problems faced.

You suffer in that many of your directors and trustees are amateurs and dilettantes, put in positions of authority for other reasons than their expertise in administration, fund raising and public relations. And yet your organization is vying for public support with experts in the field of winning public support for causes, profit and non-profit. You have a role in helping to assure that your directors and trustees are knowledgeable about essential fundamentals.

Many of you are handicapped by frequent changes in your leadership. Changes yearly or so make for a lack of continuity in policies and programs. You have a role in attempting to effect sound leadership for your organization.

You also suffer from having only limited funds in carrying on with the four M's on which accomplishment in this country depends—mindpower, manpower, mechanics and money.

Many of your problems are known to you. But I am sure many are unknown because in most cases no intensive scientific public opinion research has been made to ensure adjustment in what you do and say relative to public trends, attitudes and motivations.

There is no magic solution to meeting the problems you face. But I have found an engineering approach, planned and integrated, may help you greatly to improve your position and assure continued viability.

Thirty-three years ago the *Annals of the Academy of Political and Social Science* published my piece "The Engineering of Consent," based on the Thomas Jeffersonian principle that in our democratic society every activity must respond to and depend on the consent of the people. I used the word engineering to emphasize the organized planned approach essential to cope in the complex society we live in.

The engineering of consent has eight points in its program. I have used this approach for a variety of causes over the last three decades successfully.

1. Define your goals.
2. Carry on research to find out whether goals are attainable and how.
3. Modify your goals if research finds them unrealistic.
4. Strategy—how to use the four M's in combination.
5. Organization to carry on your public relations activity.
6. Themes and appeals.
7. Timing and planning your tactics.
8. Budget to carry out your public relations activity.

I now discuss them in greater detail.

Goals

The United Way defines its goals clearly and distinctly. X million dollars by Y date. Your problem is more complex. You need to define your goals in a variety of ways. By time goals, immediate, intermediate and long-term. What do you want to be doing at the end of each time period, and with whom and with whose support? How much mindpower, manpower, money and mechanics will you need for accomplishing these goals, and for what purposes will they be used?

Make goals as specific as possible. For instance, "out of the trenches by Christmas" is a more meaningful goal than "let's have peace."

To assure that goals are attainable and not simply unfulfilled desire requires research of the publics you depend on. Research will assure that you are meeting the public's needs and desires and also that you will know the public's attitudes and motivations so that you can win their support.

Research

Today public opinion research is practically an applied social science. Results are accurate, within a few percentage points of reality. You can retain professional researchers, if you can afford them, like Gallup, Roper, Yankelovich, or Becker in Boston. Or you can rely on academic aid, professors at your local universities, specialists in public opinion research. Or you can read available books on the subject and direct the activity yourself with volunteers. But without research you will be moving without a compass.

Research of your public is carried out in several ways. Questionnaires by mail, telephone or in-person sampling of your publics on actuarilly sound principles. You will find out areas of knowledge, ignorance towards your activity and its goals, and what elements of adjustment and maladjustment must be met by action. You will ascertain attitudes and motives of your publics.

You can also research experts in your special field to find out how they accomplish their goals. You can write to experts to ascertain what they think of your goals. You can read the literature on how other groups like yours have reached their goals.

Your feedback will tell you whether your goals are realistic or unrealistic and how to reach realistic goals.

Modification of Goals

If your research indicates your goals are unrealistic, modify them and your planned course of action to assure meeting goals.

Strategy

Your research will help you with your strategy. Strategy differs from tactics. It indicates in what combinations to use your resources of mindpower, manpower, mechanics and money. You may be carrying on a blitzkrieg or a longtime educational activity, or both. It will also give you priorities.

Organization

Organization includes the executive structure, the personnel in and out of the office to carry out your goals. This includes members of your board and the entire personnel of your organization that has or potentially has an impact on your viability.

Organization also includes your resources in library facilities. Certainly you will need current books on your specific field of action, books on strategy and tactics of winning public support, directories of manifold media. The Public Relations Society of America has comprehensive bibliographies on public relations available.

Good organization also means planning ahead with purveyors. You will also want to develop systems outlines for events, luncheons, dinners and routine activities. Manuals of this kind make for more effective functioning.

Themes and Appeals

These will also stem from research. They must meet the desires of your publics. They are directed to individuals, to sub groups and overall publics. Often they should be validated by authority, factual evidence, reasons, tradition and emotion. Psychologists and advertising men and women should be asked to help you formulate them.

Timing and Planning of Tactics

It is sound to write a complete statement of your goals, research, organization, themes and appeals and strategy so as to make the most effective use of your resources—a campaign plan, a blueprint of action.

You have available all channels of communication to your publics that you can muster. These run the gamut from letters to public service advertising to a speakers bureau with volunteers that carry your messages, to luncheon clubs and public forums, to radio and TV.

You can also develop what I call created circumstances, like celebrations of some past great from Florence Nightingale's birthday to the celebration of William Booth's founding of the Salvation Army.

In planning and timing your tactics make up three charts, one for the immediate period, another for the intermediate period and the third for the long-term period. Plan your activities in advance in accord with the research, strategy and themes and appeals decided upon. These charts will provide you with action programs for the three time periods.

Your intermediate and long-term charts are subject to change if conditions change drastically. But usually changes in the United States are gradual. Remember, for instance, that despite recession and depression the U.S. has grown at the rate of four percent annually and presumably will continue to do so.

In planning tactics, remember that advisory committees may

provide mindpower and manpower. Look for coincidences of interest that will save you money and increase your effectiveness. A public utility company may, for instance, insert your printed matter in their bills.

Budget

Your budget, even with inflation, can be planned ahead to meet your three time goals.

An engineering approach should save money and get you more money. It should increase your competitive approach to the potential dollar. It applies engineering principles to your worthy cause.

Fall 1979

As guest editor of this Fall 1979 issue of Public Relations Quarterly, ELB solicited the opinions of 27 of the nation's business leaders regarding the social significance of public relations.

The Case for Licensing and Registration for Public Relations

Today unqualified individuals can call themselves public relations practitioners. And, unfortunately, often do to the detriment of the public and the profession alike. The term is in the public domain and those who are unqualified by training, education or ethics can assume the appellation. This is not true of the term medical doctor, certified public accountant, lawyer or other profession. Society requires their licensing and registration as a protection of the public interest and all concerned.

What follows presents the case for licensing and registration, the reasons for it, the factual evidence that demands it, the historical precedence for it. It also answers questions raised about it.

First as to a definition of public relations, so that we may understand each other. In 1923, in *Crystallizing Public Opinion,* I defined the profession. The public relations practitioner advises on the relationships between a unit and the publics on which the unit depends for viability. The revolution in people power, transportation, communication and technology has brought about the need for a societal technician to deal with these new problems.

Counsel on public relations first evaluates adjustments or maladjustments between the principal's social goals and his publics. He recommends necessary changes of attitudes and actions, based on the research. He then aids principal in interpreting the principal to the publics concerned. The task embraces advice on adjustment, persuasion and information.

Today, by definition, public relations is a profession. It is an art applied to a science, social science, in which the public interest and not money, is the primary consideration. It has the earmarks of a profession—educational courses, a literature of over 15,000 items, voluntary associations and well defined codes of ethics. It lacks only state registration and licensing, a characteristic of other professions.

Over the last half century public relations has gained general acceptance, in the United States and throughout the free world, by education, government, business, social service and other sectors of the society. But, public relations as a profession today faces serious problems as to its future. The present day meaning of the two words, public relations, has become almost perjorative, due in great part that the two words are in the public domain. Anyone can call himself or herself a public relations practitioner and often does. A visiting card I was given recently illustrates the point. It has the words Public Relations across the top. The next two lines have the individual's name and address. The next line reads "How to get money for almost any purpose." Two columns below this read as follows "Venture capital, Corporate images, Executive resumes, VIP introductions, Prestige developed, Refinancing, Annual Reports, Personal Publicity, Start Your Own Business, Your Book Published."

In the United States the meaning of words has the nature of fine lace and soap bubbles, as opposed to France where a French Academy defines the meaning of words and maintains the purity of the language. Since anyone can use the term public relations, many without qualifications are lured to the activity by money. Nixon's henchmen who called themselves public relations men without justification exacerbated the problem.

To avoid negative attitudes, some public relations people practicing public relations have used other nomenclature to describe their activity, hoping in this way to avoid the perjorative meaning attached to the words public relations—Public Affairs, Community Relations, Public Communications. This has only compounded the mixed-up situation. Obviously, any nomenclature is subject to similar deflation.

Today the public, on which the future of public relations as a profession depends, has no clear cut definition of the term. They know that medical doctors, lawyers, accountants are defined by the state, are registered and licensed by the state and have to pass an examination on their education, training and character. They also know that economic sanctions apply when they are disbarred due to transgressions of one kind or another.

Obviously, this does not apply to accreditation by voluntary associations. Such accreditation carries with it no economic sanctions. The continuity of public relations demands that society and profession alike be protected against unqualified practitioners.

Incidentally, the history of western society validates such action. An increasingly complex society over the last centuries developed a need for experts and specialists to cope with the needs of society. Science, invention, technology, speeded-up communication and transportation helped bring about this need.

Early Trends

Until the Reformation, society was simple. The Church was the dominant factor. Only a few professions like medicine and law functioned independently of the Church. Organized into guilds, they kept untrained people from the field, a kind of closed shop.

With the Reformation, the Church, which had dominated society, gave up much of its power. A middle class of merchants, manufacturers and farmers developed. They provided new markets for services of specialized groups of practitioners.

Science and invention developed new professions. Architects, civil, mechanical and other kinds of engineers developed. The age of the expert and specialist was coming into being.

With the arrival of the Industrial Revolution in the early 19th century, the English government recognized the damage that could be done by unscrupulous or incompetent practitioners in various fields of activity. "Reform, train, evaluate, inspect" became a Victorian battle cry.

The United States followed suit.

Licensing in U.S.

The first state to register and license dentistry did so in 1868, pharmacy in 1874, veterinary medicine in 1886, accountancy 1896, architecture 1877. By 1894, 21 states required registration and licensing before permitting medical practice.

The 20th century accelerated the practice of licensing and the registration of professions. Today, it is nationwide.

Under this procedure, a state board of examiners from the profession is appointed. Requirements of character, education, training and experience are set up. An applicant who passes them may practice. If the code of conduct is not adhered to by the practitioner, the state may exert economic sanctions, withdrawing the practice privilege.

Accreditation by a voluntary association does not carry with it economic sanctions. Indeed, a disbarred individual may continue to call himself a public relations practitioner, for instance, and continue to practice. Nor does voluntary accreditation by an association protect the honorable practitioner from a non-association member who calls himself a public relations practitioner, though incompetent and unethical.

ELB, 1982, by noted photographer Jamie Cope.

Answers to Opposition

I believe in open covenants openly arrived at. Let me list some of the things people say against licensing and registration and answer these objections.

Some say public relations activity cannot be defined. We defined it in 1923. The definition is still sound. Leading encyclopedias carry the definition. An individual who passes an examination based on knowledge of human relations, social sciences, how to advise on adjustment, how to persuade and inform, as set by the Board of Examiners, defines the term.

Some object to government intervention as a threat to public relations. This is poppycock. Government was instituted to protect the people. Government in the case of licensing and registration protects the people from unscrupulous practitioners and protects the profession too. This method has proven itself for more than a hundred years. There may still be deviants from the standards set by law in certain cases, as has occurred in the practice of medicine and law. But the standards set by law prevail.

Some say that registration and licensing may interfere with freedom of expression of the practitioner. This is preposterous, too. This freedom is guaranteed to all Americans by the Constitution. Registered and licensed lawyers don't hesitate to speak out without fear or favor.

Some say registration and licensing will make the profession a closed corporation and exclude able men and women. This is imaginary. Anyone who qualifies may practice.

Some say it is up to members of the society to protect themselves against unscrupulous practitioners. This deprecates the duty of the state to society and the profession.

Some say wait—the time has not arrived as yet. Wait until education catches up. But in actuality university education in public relations suffers from a cultural time lag. Public relations is largely taught in colleges of journalism and mass communication or business administration. In these schools, public relations remains secondary and ancillary to the main subjects taught. Skills in writing are emphasized instead of emphasis on the social sciences. Accreditation is left to a journalism education committee. It is as if a committee of surgical instrument manufacturers accredited the curriculum of a school for surgeons.

It is my considered opinion that public relations deserves its own curriculum, based on the behavioral sciences and ethics, with communications in a secondary role. I envisage public relations as a separate field of study drawing on the many disciplines taught in the varied colleges of a university. Registration and licensing of public relations practitioners should hasten education's meeting the needs of the society. It is one way of speeding up education's lag. One additional point. When registration and licensing is instituted, the so-called grandfather clause prevails. Present practitioners continue to call themselves by the title they use. New public relations practitioners need to pass examinations before permission is granted by the state to practice.

Arguments in favor of this action are overwhelming. It protects the society and the profession. It provides standards of performance. It defines the term with state economic sanctions. It serves a useful purpose from providing a societal technician to bringing about a more balanced and adjusted society.

Fall 1979

Gaining Professional Status for Public Relations

Much discussion and planning is being carried on in high public relations circles—and justly so—to gain professional status and recognition for the practice of public relations. The gaining of status and recognition for the profession would safeguard the public and profession alike. It would prevent individuals without prerequisite education, training, experience and character to practice and cast discredit on the profession as a whole. It would obviate public relations practitioners choosing other appellations for their activity to avoid the perjorative connotations of "public relations" in some quarters.

The words "public relations practitioners" or "public relations counsel" are in the public domain. Anyone can use them for self description. Contrary to the words "lawyer," "medical doctor," "accountant," and a host of other professions, all sorts of people can call themselves "public relations practitioners" or "counsel on public relations." This has led to much abuse and to much misunderstanding that has hurt the profession and public alike.

In the case of other professions, the meaning and use of the appellation is defined by law, restricted to those who have the necessary qualifications validated by law. Economic sanctions prohibit continued use of the appellation if the individual who has been given the right to use it deviates in action from the definitions laid down. Doctors, lawyers and other professionals recognized by law are disbarred or subject to disbarment if they deviate from the standards provided by law.

Proponents of professionalism for public relations do not have to find undiscovered territory. There is a voluminous literature in English that covers the professions, at any good library.* These books analyze the professions, their development, the reasons for their growth, their organizations and their place in society, their attributes and their relations to the social structure, and their relations to higher education. Proponents of professionalism would do well to study this literature and apply the experience of other professions to gain status and recognition for the field of public relations.

They will find that to accomplish their goal demands only the simple process of gaining licensing and registration by the state, as is the case with other professions.

Reading how other professions have brought about their fulfillment of status and recognition indicates that simple steps can accomplish the ends sought.

1. Define the profession. This has often been done. As long ago as 1923, I had a definition in *Crystallizing Public Opinion.*

2. Indicate the educational requirements requisite. This too has already been done by the voluntary public relations organizations, which accredit their members.

3. Indicate the experience necessary before an individual is recognized as qualified to take the examination for practitioner.

4. Determine standards of ethical conduct. These, too, have been set up by the voluntary organizations in public relations. They would now be set up by the state, with economic sanctions of

disbarment to transgressors.

It would be possible to get one state to adopt the plan. A Board of Examiners from that state made up of outstanding practitioners of public relations would carry out a law that had been passed, based on comparable procedures now used for lawyers, medical doctors and other professions. Examinations would be given to those who qualify and if they passed the examination they would be permitted to practice and to call themselves public relations practitioners or counsel on public relations.

After one state had adopted the plan, a bandwagon pattern would undoubtedly develop and other states would follow suit to ensure the advantages of such licensing and registration.

One important element in this procedure would be that no existing practitioners of public relations, whether their use of the term is justified or not, would be subject to the legislation. Our study of other professions indicates that a so-called grandfather clause holds. And no present practitioner would be required to take the examination that new practitioners have to take. The future of public relations as a recognized profession with status will be ensured by state licensing and registration.

Summer 1980

---

*See *The Culture of Professionalism,* p. 87, Burton T. Bledstein, W. W. Norton & Company, Inc., New York

Do Our
Educational Facilities
Meet Our Needs?

Every profession's future depends on the adequacy of educational facilities available to oncoming generations. That is as true of public relations as of medicine, law and other professions, vocations practiced as an art applied to a science, in which the public interest, rather than pecuniary reward, is the primary consideration.

Do our educational facilities meet the needs of public relations of the future? Important studies of this subject have been made in the United States and other countries. Only recently, the International Public Relations Association at a conference in China discussed worldwide public relations education for the future.

I shall make recommendations on what I think is the most desirable educational preparation for public relations practice in the United States.

Public relations by definition is a profession. The public relations practitioner advises a principal, client or employer on attitudes and actions to be taken towards the publics on whom viability and fulfillment of the principal's goals depend. Principals, to survive, must understand their publics—their hopes, desires, attitudes, motivations. The public relations practitioner by research evaluates the adjustments and maladjustments between the principal's social goals and publics. The practitioner then counsels the principal on modification of goals, advises on attitudes and actions that need change. The practitioner outlines strategy, organization, themes and appeals and planning and timing of tactics to accomplish long-term, intermediate and short-term goals. Tactics include counsel to the principal in interpretation of the service, ideas or objects to the publics concerned. But the process of communication is secondary and ancillary to more basic considerations to adjustment by action.

The practitioner is a societal technician, applying the findings of the social sciences to the problem at hand. And that is what education must prepare for.

Dr. Albert Walker's report on Status and Trends of Public Relations Higher Education made for the Foundation for Public Relations Research and Education proves the need for drastic change and points up the great cultural time lag this education suffers from.

The implication is strong, Dr. Walker reports, that public relations students are drilled primarily in writing, editing and print media skills, that texts and other source materials are written chiefly by practitioners from a practical point of view. At most universities, public relations is treated as another journalistic field along with advertising, magazine journalism, photographic journalism, broadcast and electronic journalism and newspapers.

I agree with Hunter P. McCartney of the University of West Virginia quoted in the Walker report: Public relations education is hampered by too close affiliation with journalism programs and control by sometimes unsympathetic media-oriented deans. It needs to be a separate school or in an established college within an arts and science college (or social science). It should not be in a business school, in a journalism school or in any other specialized area.

Our recommendation is that universities set up independent public relations centers that call on various colleges and departments for relevant courses, and that, similar to law and medicine, only graduate degrees be given. Preparatory courses in colleges would emphasize liberal arts.

Graduate courses should cover the social sciences—psychology, social psychology, anthropology, sociology, theory and practices of all social sciences that apply to public relations.

We urge the public relations profession and public relations teachers to aid in bringing about licensing and registration. Universities will then adapt to society's needs. Society and profession alike will be safeguarded.

Winter 1980

Public relations students at Drake University, Des Moines, Iowa, with ELB after he addressed the public relations community at the university.

The PR Proficiency of the Reagan Administration

This short piece appraises the proficiency of the Reagan administration in professional public relations thinking and action. Indications to date show the administration has little knowledge or understanding of modern day public relations—what I call the engineering of consent—first outlined in my article in the *Annals of the American Academy of Political and Social Science* (March 1947). It embraces modern day strategies and tactics to carry out the Jeffersonian principle that consent of the people is essential for leadership in a democratic society. It embraces the problems involved in leading the people where they want to go.

Nonprofit and profit organizations today practice professional public relations, based on the coincidence of the public and the private interest. Certainly our government should not suffer from a cultural time lag in the use of modern public relations principles and practices employed by other institutions of the society.

Even before this article, I pointed out in a piece in the *Independent* (May 1928), "Putting Politics on the Market," the cultural lag that existed then. I wrote that politics had failed in keeping up with business methods in dealing with the public: "Politicians who know political strategy and who can develop campaign issues, who can devise strong planks for platforms and envisage broad policies cannot be given the responsibility of selling ideas to a public of more than 100,000,000. Big business is conducted on the principle that it must prepare its policies carefully and that in selling an idea to the large buying public of America it must proceed according to broad plans."

As to engineering of consent, neglected by the present administration, this has eight basic elements.

1. Defining of goals—longtime, intermediate, short-term.
2. Research to find their attainability and how.
3. Modification of goals, if research so dictates.
4. Strategy on how to use the four M's, mind-power, man and woman power, mechanics and money.
5. Organization.
6. Themes and appeals; and modification of action as indicated by the research.
7. Timing and planning of tactics.
8. Budget.

In his pre-election promises and his keynote TV speech, Reagan set goals on tax cutting and spending to right the economy.

But as early as March 6 the front page Washington Wire column in the *Wall Street Journal* began, "Worry grows that foreign side shows hurt Reagan's economic push." It stated that some presidential advisers fear that emphasis on El Salvador diverts attention from the campaign for tax and spending cuts and could lead to damaging delay. Haig's April trip to the Middle East might add to the problem, the article said.

An article in the *New York Times* on March 8 confirms the Reagan administration is proceeding on wrong premises. The article says Reagan advisers argue that Reagan is giving the people the foreign and domestic policies they voted him in for.

The administration policy advisers forget that only 52 percent of the eligible voters voted in the last election. Reagan's vote represented only 26 percent of the eligible vote. Some 47 percent of eligible voters did not vote.

Reagan and his administration represent a minority majority. Polling results taken recently by Louis Harris, respected pollster, indicate that they are misjudging their mandate. Harris' polls indicate that Americans want no prayers in public schools 50%-47%. They don't want religion taught in schools 50%-47%. They do want abortions to continue 62%-34%. They don't want to ban sex education in schools 52%-46%. They want handgun control 67%-32%. They are in favor of ERA 52%-47%. They are in favor of affirmative action 66%-24%. The public is apparently way ahead of its so-called leaders.

Certainly, with these realities, it would appear to me that the Reagan administration should tread carefully in the future. Some bright Democrat might commission George Gallup, Louis Harris or some other pollster to find out why 47% of the eligible voters did not vote in the last election and also what would make them vote in the next. Then the said Democrat would add some of the sound democratic reasons why they did not vote to the next Democratic platform, and the 26% Reagan vote would go down to defeat.
Spring 1981

Public Dissatisfaction
With Institutions

Opinion polls indicate that in the last few years public confidence of the people of the United States in the leaders of their institutions has declined markedly. The public today demands more social performance from large and small institutions, profit and non-profit. For instance, among the challenges to business of public concern are size, wealth, political influence, product reliability, truth in advertising, equal opportunity, sex discrimination, health and safety in the work place, air, water and waste pollution. Inflation, high prices, and public visibility of transgressions of businesses intensify public dissatisfactions. Public demands cannot be ignored by business. Or, for that matter, by any institution in this country, profit and non-profit.

No one doubts the strength of people power and dependence for survival on this great force. Every institution in this country must adjust to its publics so that mutual understanding is brought out. This means carefully thought out planning and action to win public support.

No one any longer is an island unto himself. We are all part of a whole. Every institution can apply what my professional partner and my wife, Doris Fleischman Bernays, lately deceased, and I learned in 58 years of working together on the public relations problems of varied clients, large and small, profit and non-profit.

Our recommendations for these clients were based on an analysis of present public attitudes towards these organizations and individuals. We then made recommendations on modifications of their attitudes and actions to meet the goals set. We also attempted to analyze possible future actions of the public as a guide to their action. Emphasis was placed on action. Words were ancillary to action.

Emphasis of our public relations activity was put on action of the client. Over the years this broad idea gained acceptance. Those within the profession and many outside recognized the need for this new profession.

As the social sciences developed and social science found out more and more about human behavior, the practice of counsel on public relations became the art of applying to human situations the findings of social scientists. It became a profession in which an art was applied to a science. Other earmarks of a profession developed. The literature grew, associations in the field proliferated, codes of ethics were propounded. Education facilities were provided by universities and colleges. But there was one element missing. The words "public relations" were in the public domain. Plumbers or car salesmen could call themselves public relations practitioners. And many who were enticed by the monetary rewards of the field started practice without responsibility to professional standards or the public.

Words in this country have the stability of soap bubbles and fine lace. So that soon public relations lost its true meaning. It became so pejorative when the Nixon henchmen called themselves public relations practitioners that many in the field adopted other names for themselves—forgetting that those names too were subject to change without notice, if anyone misused them in a way that would get public visibility.

To indicate how widespread this ignorance of the true meaning of the term public relations is, here are some examples.

One distinguished professor of public opinion research at Boston University's School of Public Communication, Dr. George A. Gitter, in a survey of undergraduate students in public relations found that none of them knew that counseling was a component of public relations practice. Only 7 percent of the graduate students in public relations knew this.

Another example: *The Public Relations Journal* of the Public Relations Society of America treats the field of public relations as if it were a euphemism for press agent, flackery, publicity. Social sciences and their application to the behavior of organizations and individuals are hardly mentioned. The emphasis is on the techniques of communications. And this in the face of findings by the social sciences that people by and large believe of what they read or hear only what they previously had believed.

Another example, most widespread in its ignorance. Advertisements appear throughout the U.S. that show no understanding of the term public relations. Here is a typical one from the *Boston Globe* of July 5, 1981. St. Margaret's Hospital advertises for a "Public Relations Coordinator." And the functions: communications professional with flair for publications, photography and audio-visual presentations needed to fill an opening.

Certainly it is high time for leaders in the profession to safeguard the future of their profession. The way to do this is to bring about licensing and registration by the state and let economic sanctions by the state be invoked to ensure ethical professional practice.

Summer 1981

62 Years in
Public Relations

In November, I was the beneficiary of three birthday parties celebrating my ninetieth birthday (I was born on November 22, 1891). One was attended by seven hundred members of the Public Relations Society of America at their 1981 convention in Chicago. Another was given by the Committee of Ninety, organized and chaired by Paul A. Newsome, founder of Newsome & Company, Boston's leading public relations organization; vice chairman Frank LeBart, 2nd vice president of the John Hancock Mutual Life Insurance Company, a director of the PRSA; John Herbert, president of the Quincy Cooperative Bank; and Frank J. Zeo, consultant. A third was held at the Rotary Club of Boston, chaired by Mr. Zeo, a former president of the Club, addressed by Marcelle Farrington, new president of the New England chapter of the PRSA, Mr. LeBart and Mr. Herbert. I figure the total attendance at these three events was in the neighborhood of 1300. I naturally am much gratified by this extraordinary support of public relations.

A ninetieth birthday is a good time to look backward and forward, into the future, to appraise the state of the profession. After all, I have spent 69 years of my working life in some form dealing with the public. For eight years after graduation from

Cornell University in 1912, I was engaged in various public oriented activities; as editor of the Dietetic and Hygienic Gazette and staff member of the Medical Review of Reviews; as coproducer of a Broadway play; as publicity man for Broadway dramatic productions, Caruso and other musical stars, the Diaghileff Russian Ballet and Nijinsky; and as a staff member of the United States Committee on Public Relations in New York and at the Peace Conference in Paris after World War I.

I have spent 62 years in counsel on public relations. When I returned from Paris in 1919 I decided to apply my wartime experience with the Committee on Public Information to peacetime pursuits. During the war, we worked to build understanding of war aims among the American people, to win over the neutrals, strengthen our allies' morale and break down the enemy's. I opened an office in New York City and enlisted a young woman, Doris E. Fleischman, whom I later married and worked with for 58 years. There was nowhere to go for information or advice on our contemplated activity. There were no educational courses, no books, no association.

At first we called our activity "publicity direction." We intended to give advice to clients on how to direct their actions to get public visibility for them. But within a year we changed the service and its name to "counsel on public relations." We recognized that all actions of a client that impinged on the public needed counsel. Public visibility for one action of a client might be vitiated by another not in the public interest. We took the word "counsel" from the law. The words public relations, we found out later, had been used in the 1830's to mean action for the general good. Then they had dropped out of sight. The two words were again used in the trade press of public utilities and other industries attacked by muckrakers in the early twentieth century to describe the work of the newsmen hired by those attacked to "whitewash" them. But the two words never reached the broad public.

The first thing we did to advance the new profession was to write a book, *Crystallizing Public Opinion*, to outline its scope, function and ethics, published in 1923 by Boni and Liveright. It is still in print. The second was to induce New York University to give a course on the subject in the same year.

And today, 62 years later, public relations is a profession, recognized and spread over the free world. The International Public Relations Association headed by Sam Black has some 660 members in over sixty countries. The Public Relations Society of America has over ten thousand members. There are other public relations associations in varied fields. The literature covers some 16,000 items. There are educational courses at institutions of higher learning all over the free world. The United States lacks only licensing and registration to fulfill a profession's full requirement.

Certainly the 34th National Conference of the Public Relations Society of America demonstrated the profession has come of age. *Public Relations News* reported an audience of 1527 assembled in Chicago. Enthusiasm was evident throughout the conferences outlined in detail in a 52-page program.

As to the future, as long as democratic society lasts, the public relations profession will grow. Mutual understanding is basic to society's well being. Advice and counsel based on the social sciences will grow.

Public relations counseling should continue a great safeguard of a free democratic competitive society, in which people power remains dominant.

Fall 1981

Advertising Agencies,
Stay Out of
Public Relations!

A question of vital importance to the future of public relations in the United States is currently agitating the members of the
profession: whether the present move of large advertising agencies
buying up and taking over independent public relations organizations is good or bad for the future of the public relations profession
and for the public.

This subject was discussed at the June meeting of the New
England chapter of the Public Relations Society of America (at
which Cindy Strousse, APR was elected president of the 30-year-
old association). An indication of the high concern in the subject by
public relations practitioners was shown by the 145 attendants at
the meeting, of the 250 membership association. The pros and cons
of the issue were presented by the speakers, who represented public
relations organizations and combined advertising-public relations
organizations.

Certainly, according to this observer, with 63 years of practice in
the field, such takeovers serve neither the interests of the public
relations profession nor the public interest. Let me tell you why.

When the profession of public relations was first outlined in my book, *Crystallizing Public Opinion,* published by Boni and Liveright, Inc. in 1923, it was envisioned as other professions functioned: that is, as an art applied to a science, in this case social science, and in which the primary motivation was the public interest and not pecuniary motivation. An ethical public relations firm is governed by this principle. It does not, for instance, take on clients who do not serve the public interest; for instance, we turned down Franco's Spain and Somaza's Nicaragua.

An advertising agency, on the other hand, is not a profession. It is strictly a business, governed by the bottom line. It can accept its seventeen percent from any client who functions within the law. Public relations organizations are and should be governed in their actions by the public interest. No reputable public relations organization would today accept a cigarette account, since their cancer-causing effects have been proven. Advertising agencies are governed by the bottom line, a highly persuasive force in business.

As long as 48 years ago, in 1934, Stanley Walker in his book, *City Editor* (Frederick A. Stokes Company), the then-city editor of the *New York Tribune* noted adaptations that advertising agencies were making from the public relations field. He wrote, "Bernays must receive credit or blame for an important shift in the methods used by the larger advertising agencies .... A few years ago, advertising agencies devoted their attention to straight advertising. Now they have added research workers (which may be a good thing), and great numbers of thinkers, behaviorists, trend-observers, experts with chart and graph, child trainers, students of sleep and what not." Certainly there could be no objection to these additions to improve the writing and effectiveness of advertising writing and placement.

But to buy up a profession whose effectiveness must be based on independent judgments and advice to clients—based on the coincidence of the public and private interest, regardless of other consid-

erations and as independent as that of lawyers' or doctors' judgments—is not in the interest of the profession or the public. Advertising agencies buying up public relations organizations is as if a medical instrument manufacturing company took over a medical college or a law book publisher bought out a law college.
Fall 1982

Diane Cotman, partner in Strategic Thinking, Boston public relations firm, with ELB on yachting party of United Nations Association of Boston, held in Boston Bay, 1986.

The Case for Licensing PR Practitioners

Every day brings me cumulative evidence that if we want the profession of public relations to be considered a respected vocation, we had better do something drastic about it—and now. The PRSA should in its own interest and the public interest lead the way. We must get the two words, public relations, defined by law with licensing and registration of practitioners, as is the case with lawyers, medical doctors and other professionals.

Today the term "public relations" is in the public domain and anyone—many without training, education, or ethical behavior—is welcome to use it to describe what he or she professes to do. Already the term is a pejorative one in many quarters because of its exploitation by the ignorant and unscrupulous. Richard Nixon's henchmen in the Watergate scandal, among many others, helped to bring this about. Many practitioners sought other designations to identify themselves. But obviously these designations are also subject to deflation unless defined by law through licensing and registration.

Here are some examples of misuse of the term "public relations":

- Examine the help-wanted advertisements in the *Wall Street Journal* on Tuesdays and the *New York Times* on Sundays. You will see for yourself the many diversified meanings the advertiser has of the profession. I noted that one advertiser was looking for a tourist guide and stated he wanted a public relations representative.

- I have before me a letter from a model agency, offering services of Vicki for my next trade fair as my public relations representative. Vicki is described in the letter as the leading public relations representative for the *Penthouse* publishing empire. The letter tells me her combination of good looks, ability and warmth makes her a truly unique personality.

- I have in my files a business card passed on to me by a self-anointed public relations practitioner. It is typical of the looseness with which the term is used by many. The first line of the card gives his name. The second states his vocation "Better Public Relations," the next two lines his address. The next line reads "How to get money for almost any purpose." Then come two columns. The first reads Venture Capital, Corporate Images, Executive Resumes, VIP Introductions, Prestige Developed. The second column reads Refinancing, Annual Reports, Personal Publicity, Start Your Own Business, Your Book Published.

- Only recently the professor of public relations at a distinguished Boston college reported to me a guest speaker, who called herself a public relations practitioner who practices in Boston. She talked to the public relations students and told them the practice of public relations could not be taught and by all means to abstain from reading books. Only experience could benefit them.

- An article by Daniel B. Wood in the *Christian Science Monitor* started this way: "PR. The initials became almost as ignominious as the scarlet letter itself. Putting them on your letter head or business card was like hinting the return of the locust. You whispered them even to your friends.... Public relations people even changed their titles: information specialist, public affairs director, community relations manager, corporate issues director."

History validates licensing and registration for the professions. After the Reformation in England, the Church gave up sovereignty of most affairs. Trade and commerce developed. The guilds of that period demanded high standards of their members as a protection to public and the profession they represented. With the development of science and invention and a more complicated society, new professions of varied kinds arose—from engineering to architecture, accounting to dentistry. In the early 19th century, registration and licensing were carried out in Great Britain with economic sanctions and sometimes disbarment if the professional transgressed the code of ethics. This system spread to the United States where licensing and registration for professionals is now the rule, also with disbarment of transgressors.

No such safeguards prevail for public relations.

Registration and licensing would also correct a sad situation as regards public relations education in this country. Today the curriculum called public relations in the colleges and universities of this country—and the free world, for that matter—is as diversified as is the misuse of the term.

Educational requirements under the recommended licensing and registration procedures would consist of a liberal arts degree and two years' study of the social sciences culminating in a Master's degree.

Spring 1983

Closing Up the
Cultural Time Lag

In my lifetime, changes have taken place that often demanded revision of the conduct of our lives. New lifestyles were brought about by science and invention as well as by the social sciences. Some causes could be foreseen; others could not. The public had to adjust as best it could.

Over sixty years of professional activity as counsel on public relations, my wife and I often helped bridge gaps between public ignorance and public knowledge and action on these innovations. We worked with Columbia Broadcasting System at its inception in the late twenties, and then with the National Broadcasting Company, to gain acceptance for the new radio communications system. We helped gain public acceptance for television with the inventive Philco Radio and Television Corporation over fifty years ago. For the American Telegraph and Telephone Company we promoted the first international telephonic communication between Ambassador Dwight Morrow in Mexico City and his fellow citizens in New Jersey at luncheon meetings of Rotary Clubs throughout the state.

In these and other activities, we closed up cultural time lag and brought about better adjustment to these innovations among the public.

Conditions of all kinds are constantly changing in the United States. Hugo Munsterberg rightly called the United States the land of unlimited possibilities. In the 19th century American institutions did not prepare the people for change. The frontiersman was role model for the society. But today a new outlook in education prevails. The New School for Social Research in New York has led the way in adult education on a variety of subjects. New York University in response to my suggestion gave the first course in public relations, which I conducted in 1923. Men and women who worked all day came to learn at night to keep up with their times.

Today adult education plays an important role in public relations and other fields, preparing people to deal with change, past and future. Pace University, a private university in New York with over 29,000 students day and evening, is a leader in providing middle management men and women in public relations an opportunity to catch up with what they may have missed. Under the direction of Richard Newman, of the university's Professional Development Institute, and Dean James C. Hall, I recently had the exciting experience of giving a two-day seminar in Boston. Students came from California, Maryland, Washington, D.C., the Netherland Antilles, Georgia, Minnesota and elsewhere—representing activities as diversified as their employers: a medical center, U.S. Army Corps of Engineers, a wax company, religious groups, manufacturers, Blue Cross, etc.

Several weeks later, Mr. Newman invited me to participate in a comparable group, as diversified in background and home base. F. John Pessolano gave instruction in the intricacies of the computer and equipped us to handle this innovative instrument revolutionizing storage and retrieval of information.

Under Mr. Newman's direction numerous seminars will be held this summer on such subjects as Employee Internal Publications, Financial Public Relations, Government Public Affairs, Public

Information, Introductory Public Relations, Issues Management, Publicity Techniques, Media Relations, Research and Evaluation, Speechwriting.

This innovation in adult education bodes well for public relations' future—both profit and nonprofit. Middle management will understand the new developments they may have missed and will more speedily move towards top management. American organizations will be better equipped to deal with change—as will the publics on whom they are dependent. Top management should make similar efforts to avoid suffering from cultural time lag.

Summer 1983

ELB at Pace University, New York City, 1985, learning how to use the computer with Richard Newman, director of the university's Professional Development Institute.

Research and Evaluation

In 1914, some seven decades ago, I did the publicity for the Broadway production of Daddy Long Legs, which recognized the drawbacks of orphanages and the more humane care of foster parents. Publicity was a one-way street. I functioned by turning out copy and sending it to media on the basis of my limited experience, by hunch and by insight. Or I planned and consummated overt acts that made the news, in the same way.

There was no research of the relevant publics made in advance. Social science had not yet developed the scientific methods to evaluate public attitude and motivation. I tried to evaluate our audiences by standing at the box office at matinee performances and appraising the theatre goers as they walked in. I tried to decide by clairvoyance why they came to the show and what their socio-economic status was. I let that determine the publics I would try to reach and the methods of reaching them. It was a game of super-sensory perception.

Today all this is changed. The development of the social sciences in the twentieth century has brought about new revolutionary methods of appraisal of human beings. Studies of motivation, of attitudes and potential action are made today. They make my early attempts seem like fortune telling. Studies today made by competent fact finders are accurate within three percent of their findings. These new approaches have all come in seven decades. Men whom I knew at the time led the way: Claude Robinson, Paul Lazarsfeld, George Gallup, Elmo Roper. They have been followed by able successors.

Wrongly there was a common belief at the time that leaders in their special fields knew what the public's hopes, wishes and desires were and gratified them. How wrong that belief was.

My researches at the Gayety Theatre in 1914 gave me little real information or aid. But they did establish one principle I have followed throughout my professional life. It is that research is basic to any action taken in dealing with any public. The public must be studied before action is taken. We must have a base line that indicates how we are to adjust to the public, educate it and inform it.

Research in the form of public opinion polls, market research, in-depth studies of human behavior is today the rule for any sound public relations activity. In the last twenty years we have not accepted clients unless they are willing to have a research made of the public at issue or unless such figures are available elsewhere. Proceeding without a survey is like a medical doctor prescribing medicines without a thorough examination of the patient.

The reasons for research are simple. The people of our country are made up of diverse backgrounds. This is true of the over three hundred million men, women and children of the United States as it is of a neighborhood. Their attitude, knowledge, apathy, ignorance, and expertise towards specific ideas, services, products, whatever, vary. These differences may depend on many causes—socio-economic status, knowledge, ignorance, apathy, education, sex, age, other causes. It would be foolhardy in the light of today's understanding of sociology and social psychology to proceed with any publics without first making a study of them.

We know from a study of man through the ages and from our

own history as a nation that the past is prelude to the future. People as a rule will retain the attitudes and actions the research reveals, unless some revolutionary activity changes them. We must remember that we live in a speeded up, rapidly changing world. Despite basic continuity it is subject to change without notice as science and invention or some new idea or concept modifies public attitudes and action. I have noted in my lifetime earthshaking innovations in communication and transportation that have modified perceptions and attitudes of people: radio, television, cable television, airplane, national newspapers, computers. And that is true in other areas as well. The atom bomb is one example. Medical research is another. New drugs have changed attitudes and actions of those who might otherwise have had different habits. Insulin, Salvarsan, coumarin, nitroglycerin have modified the attitudes and actions of people who respond to them.

Evaluating services should be made from time to time to find out whether public relations activities that have been attempted have been successful, as well as to note whether any other changes have taken place. In some cases such evaluations might be made every six months. Or they may be accelerated by some unexpected happening. Certainly such evaluations should be carried out.

The basic truth is self-evident—that research and evaluation are essential in any program of public relations that attempts at sound public relationships over a period of time.

Winter 1983

Old People

An issue of national importance, ignored and neglected, is coming to the fore. Every public relations practitioner will have to face it and know how to deal with it. Inevitable forces moving at a rapid rate will soon give it widespread national public visibility. The issue will continue to grow in time. It covers many fields: economic, government relations, health, human rights, employment practices, medical research, housing and a host of others. Public relations activities will and should play an important role in the solution of this vital issue.

I refer to the problems involved in the rapid expansion of the aging population in the United States. The 1983 report of the Carnegie Corporation states the problem succinctly in a paragraph titled "Public Policy Implications of an Aging Society." It reads:

> An unprecedented change in the age composition of the United States population is taking place. The median age is now 31 and rising. The number of persons below the age of 13 has dropped by nearly 7 million since 1970, while the number of adults age 25 to 34 has grown by over 13 million and of the elderly by more than 6 million. By the next century, fully 12 to 15 percent of the population will be 65 years or older, a figure that will rise to 20 percent by about the year 2035.

Here are some additional pertinent facts from a "fact sheet on agism":

- Over 23 million Americans are past 65 years of age.

- Government figures say that eight out of ten older Americans are in good health and capable of work.
- Three million people over 65 are still working—but half of them are self-employed.
- Like all types of discrimination, agism is based on myths, not facts.

The public policy changes resulting from the changes that have taken place in the American population are tremendous and every practitioner in public relations had better prepare himself or herself to cope with them.

In my own case (I am now 93) I was not aware of the problems of agism until some thirty years ago when Mayor Robert Wagner appointed me chairman of a senior citizens committee to make New Yorkers aware of the problems of aging. I was so ignorant of the issue that I did what I always did when confronted by a problem I knew little about. I called up Columbia University, asked for a professor versed in the specific subject, in this case gerontology, and asked for the name of the most authoritative book on the subject. Then I bought a copy of the book and had a graduate student abstract it and furnish me with the abstract the next morning. I then probably knew more about the subject than the executive I was talking to because he was too busy to read books.

For my senior citizenship query I was given University of Chicago professor George Havighurst's book, titled *Gerontology.*

Next morning I learned proven facts most Americans are not aware of which changed my life and I think will change yours. If these facts were generally known and accepted I think they would go a long way in changing the attitudes of most Americans—which would help in dealing with and solving and resolving some of the problems the United States faces in dealing with the aging population.

Havighurst states that, contrary to the popular belief that all of us have only one age—chronological—we all have five ages and they do not necessarily match: a chronological age, a physiological age, a mental age, a societal age, and an emotional age.

Shakespeare was in error when he wrote of the seven progressive ages of man—from the infant, puking and mewling in the nurse's arms to the old man decrepit, sans sight, sans hearing, sans everything.

Obviously, our societal structure has been built on fallacious beliefs about agism. Bismarck, chancellor of the new German Empire, told Kaiser Wilhelm that 65 was the age to discharge employees, and we practice it in this country without rhyme or reason.

I think it is in the public interest, convenience and necessity that public relations practitioners deepen their own understanding of the personal, professional and social complexities of an aging population—as well as actively contribute to public understanding.
Fall 1984

Massachusetts Governor Michael Dukakis greeting ELB in the State House. With them are Frank Zeo (left), management consultant, and Richard Rowland, Massachusetts Secretary of Elder Affairs.

Let's Exclude the Incompetent and Unqualified from Public Relations

Recently in Washington, D.C. I was the dinner guest of the executive board of the National Capital Chapter of the Public Relations Society of America. The dinner took place the night before I was to give a talk before the chapter members at the Capital Hilton hotel.

I thought the occasion offered a good opportunity to find out from my fellow guests the most important problems confronting the public relations profession now and in the future, as a basis for my talk the next day.

Paul S. Forbes, president of the chapter, and his associates, Alvin M. Hattel and other members of the board, participated with other guests in the lively discussion that lasted until ten-thirty p.m.

I was most gratified that the major points of the discussion centered on defining for themselves, their clients or employers, for the public and the media just what public relations is and does.

It was most interesting to me as I listened to and participated in the discussion how great was our agreement on many points about public relations. We all agreed that the most pressing problems facing the entire public relations field today and tomorrow are those involved with defining the profession. And I made the subject of my talk the next day the solving of this problem of definition.

Public relations must define itself to its practitioners and to all the publics of the society, on which its present and future depend. Words in the American language's public domain have the stability of soap bubbles and are subject to constant change—words, for example, like "gay" and "people's republic." Professions like law and medicine and architecture recognized these same difficulties some hundred and fifty years ago and asked the British parliament to have their qualified members licensed and registered with legal sanctions for those who did not adhere to the code of ethics they signed. The United States adopted comparable methods.

Today if I am in a small town in Arkansas and see an M.D. sign in a window, I know at a glance that the individual has gone through a liberal arts course at a university, has then taken two years of medicine at a university, has then had special training, has passed the examination of a board of medical examiners, and has signed a code of ethics, which is enforced by legal sanctions. The latter ensures that standards of the profession are maintained.

In public relations, however, this is not the case. Any transgressor who has called himself or herself a public relations practitioner and is sent to jail—as were Nixon's associates who called themselves public relations experts—may continue in the field. The two words "public relations" consequently become pejorative. Men and women adopt other terms for what they do—public affairs director, public issues manager, community affairs manager. They may or may not be aware that these words are also in the public domain and subject to comparable change in meaning without notice.

Everywhere are obvious signs the situation needs remedying. The PRSA admits members without qualification tests. The APR degree carries no legal sanctions for transgressors.

Maybe there is a ray of light in the dark situation. *Public Relations News,* December 24, 1984, carries the news that 25 public relations world leaders, who were asked for the most pressing challenges confronting public relations professionals, stated as number 1, "Approve of licensing that will define the public relations discipline, exclude the incompetent and unqualified, and set national and international standards of public relations performance and ethics."

Winter 1984

ELB cutting birthday cake at his 93rd birthday party given by Public Relations Society of America at their annual convention in 1984.

Public Relations'
First Course and
First Book

On March 26, 1985 New York University celebrated the 62nd anniversary of the first public relations course ever given at an institution of higher learning. President John Brademas presented me with a large presidential certificate, which stated that "for outstanding services and attainments there has been entered upon the Roster of Honor of the University the award to Edward L. Bernays of this official citation with all the approbation, esteem and respect implied in such investiture."

I never anticipated such recognition when I gave that first course 62 years ago in the same Main Building of the Washington Square campus of New York University.

My wife of one year, Doris E. Fleischman, and I lived only a few doors away on Washington Mews. Having returned from the Paris Peace Conference in 1919, I served as a staff member of the U.S. Committee on Public Information, and I opened an office for the practice of publicity direction. In 1920 I changed my activity from publicity direction to counsel on public relations, a new term. I recognized a client might receive widespread public visibility from some action recommended and then deflate himself or herself by some untoward action later. All actions and attitudes needed to be considered vis-à-vis the public if identity and reputation were to be achieved and maintained. The words "counsel on public relations" expressed the function correctly.

But then the question arose of how to establish validity for the title and the profession. A newsletter, *Contact,* edited by my wife and partner, helped establish meaning for the words.

Much skepticism prevailed. The words "counsel on public relations" were regarded by some as a euphemism for press agent or publicity person.

My wife and I decided two overt actions would further the new profession.

The first was a book. I wrote *Crystallizing Public Opinion,* the first ever on public relations, which was published 1923, the same year as the first course. Boni and Liveright were the publishers. The firm, one of our first clients, was headed by Horace Liveright, a former curb broker turned literary man. He loved doing daring things.

Walter Lippman in 1922 had published *Public Opinion.* He had impressed me with his delineation of basic principles of public opinion. His book did not deal with action. My book would lay down the principles and practices and ethics of the profession and how to deal with people power and public opinion.

Some critics treated the book as if it were a euphemistic approach to publicity. Others took it as seriously as I did and regarded the new field described as a vital, promising profession. It was a real sign of recognition when H. L. Mencken in his *Supplement* to *The American Language* published my complete definition of the new profession.

A second method to establish the profession was the recognition of a great university teaching public relations. Academic status is not a purchasable commodity but is accepted because of intrinsic merit. I approached the faculty head of New York University at Washington Square. For three decades I taught the subject evenings and was made an adjunct professor. Today public relations is practiced and taught throughout the free world. But the words "public relations" are in the public domain. No educational or practice standards are legally set as in other professions like medicine and law. Their standards are maintained by licensing, registration and legal sanctions which protect the profession and the public.

But plans will soon be announced to cope with the problem, a good beginning for the next 62 years.

Spring 1985

ELB celebrating being named honorary 15 millionth visitor at the Ford Museum in Dearborn, Michigan, 1985. Bernays was counsel on public relations for the year-long celebration of the anniversary of Thomas Edison's invention of the incandescent lightbulb, which ended with a banquet in Dearborn attended by President Herbert Hoover, Henry Ford, Marie Curie, and other notables from around the world.

Operatives & Lobbyists vs. PR Professionals

Several recent events indicate the time has come for qualified public relations practitioners to insist on registration and licensing and legal sanctions for their profession.

The first is the grievous blunder of President Ronald Reagan visiting the cemetery where Nazi SS assassins are buried. Newspapers described the blunder as resulting from poor public relations advice. Any qualified public relations practitioner knows symbols are shortcuts to human understanding. Negative symbols, like swastikas, usually carry more meaning than words. Vance Packard in *The Hidden Persuaders* devoted pages to their power. Had the so-called public relations advisers known their field, the sad event would never have taken place.

This incident proves they should be qualified by education and licensing and registration before being given the appelation.

Other incidents indicate the need for licensing and registration. A headline in the *Washington Post* of April 7, 1985 demonstrates the importance of differentiating lobbying from public relations. The headline read "Partners in Political PR Firm Typify Republican New Breed." A subhead read "Operatives in Demand by Candidates, Governments." Four young men have become "a major new presence" in the capital "in connections, influence and hard-ball politics." Our U.S. constitution validates the right of petition. To call this public relations is as much of a misnomer as calling the laying on of hands to cure a disease medical practice.

An article "Playing the Access Game" in another Washington publication, *The Washington Dossier,* April 1985, further validates the necessity of defining public relations. The article tells how the PR Class of '85 (it gives names) makes a lot of money by practicing "access." They use their former government connections to give them clout. They introduce clients to politicians in high places. And get rich. The article, by Dom Bonafede, points out that the practice has drawn criticism from traditionalists in public relations and that it runs counter to the concept "envisaged by PR Pioneer Edward L. Bernays."

Certainly what is being done is not public relations. Defining the meaning of the words by law will ensure that only those will be permitted to call themselves by the term who are qualified by education and examination.

These are only a few of the incidents that have received public visibility that show how far from real public relations is what is called public relations by the media and by individuals.

H. L. Mencken, the great American philologist in his first book on the American language, referring to such euphemisms as realtor for real estate agent, mortician for undertaker, beautician for hairdresser, referred to public relations counsel as a euphemism for press agent.

But in his *Supplement* to *The American Language,* published in 1945, he printed my definition as valid. It referred to the public relations practitioner as an applied social scientist, who advised client or employer on attitudes and actions to meet his or her social goals and to conform to the hopes, aspirations and needs of the publics on whom viability depended.

Certainly the history of the profession in the last six decades has validated its needs in our society. Certainly for its own interest and for the public interest it deserves to be defined and practiced according to definition.

Summer 1985

ELB speaking with Ted Turner of Turner Broadcasting Systems at Advertising Club of Boston luncheon.

A New Campaign
Has Begun

The Public Relations Society of America prides itself on being a professional association. In its 1984 Directory on page 7 it lists its purposes, structure and services. It states that it is the major professional association for public relations formed to unite those engaged in the profession of public relations.

It states that acceptance into PRSA requires that individual members adhere to the Society's Code of Professional Standards for the Practice of Public Relations and that each PRSA member fulfill an individual responsibility to make the public relations profession worthy of public confidence.

Despite this commendable statement, public relations practice is not, by the accepted definition of the term today, a profession. This situation can be corrected, and a group of us are attempting to correct it.

Other vocations, like law and medicine, have become professions by invoking legal steps to meet the definition of a profession. Public relations should do the same.

What are the earmarks of a profession? First, a definition. A profession is an art applied to a science (in the case of public relations, a social science), in which the public interest rather than pecuniary motivation is the primary force.

Second, a literature of books that define and explain the field. From public relations' first book, *Crystallizing Public Opinion,* there is now a bibliography of over 16,000 items. But, in a true profession, the embodiment of this knowledge is *tested in examinations given by the state.* Today, no such examinations are given to that great variety of people who say they're public relations professionals.

Third, a code of ethics which practitioners must adhere to. The code carries legal sanctions. Those within the profession who do not adhere to them are subject to disbarment through legal mechanisms. Under present conditions, an unethical person can sign the code of PRSA, become a member, practice unethically—untouched by any legal sanctions. In law and medicine, such an individual is subject to disbarment from the profession.

Fourth, a true profession has associations of professional members. Today, no examinations of any kind are given to the applicant for membership in the PRSA. Two endorsements by present members and payment of dues are entitlement to membership, if the individual can read and write. Without a testing of professional standards—or a license proving that such testing has taken place—today's public relations association member is not *necessarily* a professional.

Fifth, there are educational facilities for the education of the potential practitioner of a profession. Perforce there are standard instructions, because the individual applicant to the profession needs to pass an examination set by the state board of examiners. Today, since the words "public relations" are in the public domain, there are no standards: any institution of higher learning can define public relations on its own terms.

This sad situation makes it possible for anyone, regardless of education or ethics, to use the term "public relations" to describe his or her function.

To set public relations firmly on the road to becoming a recognized profession, a number of us have formed a committee to bring about licensing and registration of public relations practitioners. Co-chairmen are myself and Ted Baron, LL.B, APR, former president of the New York PRSA chapter. Members of the committee include:

- Don Bates, APR, administrator of the PRSA Foundation
- Phyllis H. Berlowe, APR, vice president of Marketshare, a division of Doremus and Co.
- Allen Center, APR, noted author, practitioner and educator
- Paul S. Forbes, Ph.D., APR, president of the Washington, D.C. chapter of PRSA
- Frank LeBart, APR, former national secretary of PRSA
- Alan Scott, APR, professor emeritus of public relations at the University of Texas
- Fernando Valverde, APR, president of the Public Relations Society of Puerto Rico

We will carry out a campaign of education, information, and persuasion to the public and the profession alike, with a view to bringing about the acceptance of registration and legally sanctioned licensing of public relations practitioners.

It should be pointed out that in this procedure the passage of any law affects the new generation of practitioners. The grandfather clause, as it is called, prevails. Living individuals who call themselves public relations practitioners will be permitted to do so.

The procedure outlined above has its basis in the history of other professions.

Fall 1985

Public Relations
Has a New Field
to Conquer

On November 22, 1985 I celebrated my 94th birthday at my home in Cambridge, Massachusetts. Present were one hundred and ten friends, ranging in age from twenty to ninety-four. We all had a good time together from 7:30 to 1:00 a.m. It reminded me of some basic truths about age that I believe public relations practitioners may not be as aware of as they should be.

Nor do I believe that the public is aware of certain facts about age. Most people believe that every one individual has only one age—chronological—and that in this process the total individual deteriorates. Shakespeare expressed this belief in *As You Like It* when he wrote of the progressive ages of man from the infant "mewling and puking in the nurse's arms" to the decrepit old man "sans teeth, sans eyes, sans taste, sans everything."

Actually, today scientists have found that age is not necessarily progressive. We all have five ages and they don't necessarily match—chronological, physiological, mental, societal, and emotional.

Modern medicine has helped bring this about. In my lifetime, the average age of an individual has increased from 46 years when I was born in 1891 to 74 today for men and 79 for women. In the next century one-fifth of the U.S. population will be over 65. Today one in eight is over 65.

The public relations field needs to orient the American public to these facts. Today many regard the chronological age as the only one to consider. Men and women over 65 are automatically relieved of their positions. I am honorary chairman of a nonprofit organization in Boston called Careers for Later Years. We attempt to get jobs for men and women over 55 who are discriminated against because of their age. A professor of gerontology wrote me that such discrimination is as anti-American as discrimination based on sex, religion, color or ethnic origin.

Recently, as co-chairman of the Massachusetts Committee for Economic Justice for Older Workers, I helped build public support for a bill that would make it illegal for anyone to carry out mandatory retirement on the basis of age. The Massachusetts legislature passed the bill, and the governor signed it.

It seems to me to be the obligation of the field of public relations to take up the cultural time lag in the public interest. Unless this is done, everyone who is chronologically old will feel the impact of discrimination.

A recent incident dramatizes my point vividly. Claude Pepper, the distinguished congressman from Florida and an effective spokesman for the aged, celebrated his 84th birthday at the Park Sheraton Hotel in Washington, D.C. It was a fundraising dinner for studies in the sociology of aging at a Florida university, attended by hundreds of guests.

Forty well known guests over 80 years old were invited. They were taken to the mezzanine overlooking the dining room. A marine in uniform was assigned to each person to hold his or her arm while walking down the grand stairway. I thought it might be interesting to demonstrate to the guests that all chronologically aged persons did not require this. I tore myself loose from the marine assigned to me and ran precipitously down the stairs. The audience of diners, astounded, burst into applause.

The event was reported in the *Washington Post,* as if a new continent had been discovered. My physician tells me that my physiological age is 61. And this is no rare exception.

Public relations has a new field to conquer.

Winter 1985

The late Frank Manning, Massachusetts senior citizen advocate, with ELB in march before State House in Boston leading demonstration in favor of law forbidding mandatory retirement because of age. The Massachusetts law was passed in the fall of 1985.

PRPLR

The Public Relations Practitioners for Licensing and Registration of public relations practitioners is now actively functioning and the future looks very promising for the achievement of its goal to make public relations a real and recognized profession.

It might be well at this point to present the decision of the Appelate Division of the New York Supreme Court as to what a profession is. Here is that decision:

"A profession is not a business. It is distinguished by the requirements of extensive formal training and learning, admission to practice by a qualifying licensure, a code of ethics imposing standards qualitatively and extensively beyond those that prevail or are tolerated in the marketplace, a system for discipline of its members for violation of the code of ethics, a duty to subordinate financial reward to social responsibility, and notably, an obligation on its members, even in non-professional matters, to conduct themselves as members of a learned, disciplined, and honorable occupation. These qualities distinguish professionals from others whose limitations on conduct are largely prescribed only by general legal standards and sanctions, whether civil or criminal. Interwoven with the professional standards, of course, is pursuit of the ideal and that the profession not be debased by lesser commercial standards.

The first meeting of the committee was convened this past winter in my home in Cambridge, Massachusetts. As an indication of their interest, members came from New York, Memphis and Washington, D.C. to form a policy committee, which is the decision-making body of the committee. Attending the meeting were:

- Ted Baron, LL.B, APR, president of Ted Baron Inc., past president, New York chapter, PRSA
- E. W. Brody, Ed.D., APR, Memphis State University, president, Memphis chapter, PRSA
- William J. Corbett, J.D., APR, vice president for communications, American Institute of Certified Public Accountants, New York, N.Y.
- Paul S. Forbes, Ph.D., APR, Paul S. Forbes & Associates Inc., past president, National Capital chapter, PRSA, Washington, D.C.

We agreed that interested public relations practitioners are welcome to join PRPLR under the following conditions: Candidates should be accredited by PRSA or IABC, or have five years' experience and be recommended by two practitioners who are accredited. A small contribution to the treasury of PRPLR is required.

A draft of a model state licensing statute will shortly be drawn up. Promising jurisdictions for an initial effort currently appear to be Rhode Island, Connecticut, Florida and Puerto Rico.

Initial public reaction has been encouraging. I have received letters from outstanding practitioners approving our effort. The PR newsletters have featured the meeting and the activities of the committee. *PR Reporter* carried stories and has asked its readers for comment. *New England Adweek* featured a front-page story. *The Boston Herald* in a Sunday section carried a piece of mine on the importance of licensing and registration with legal sanctions, emphasizing its vital concern to the public and the field of public relations. *The Providence Journal* published a long piece on the pros and cons of licensing and registration. And so it went.

To me, there are only pros for the end goal of the committee since this is the only way for PR to become a profession.

One interesting development has occurred since the committee has been in existence. In response to my letter, Anthony Franco, the current president of PRSA, has written me that he is calling together a committee to discuss licensing and registration. Frank LeBart, APR, one of our members, will attend the meeting on our behalf.

In the meantime, the momentum of public opinion will go on to bring about the licensing and registration which I had envisioned in my book *Crystallizing Public Opinion* in 1923 and which I have fought for in the interests of public relations and the public for five decades.

Spring 1986

ELB, 1986.

Roots of Modern Public Relations: The Bernays Doctrine

By Marvin N. Olasky

Edward Bernays, 1928: "Intelligent men must realize that propaganda is the modern instrument by which they can fight for productive ends and help to bring order out of chaos."

Virtually every public relations practitioner, when asked to name the founder of modern public relations, will say: Ivy Lee. Textbooks love to quote the "Declaration of Principles" Lee sent to newspaper editors in 1906 when he was beginning his practice. "All our work is done in the open," Lee wrote, stressing his plan to "frankly and openly . . . supply to the press and public of the United States prompt and accurate information. . . . " But how much does a goody two-shoes statement of that sort reflect the reality of public relations work then or now? In practice, Ivy Lee felt compelled to publicize distortions in a way which led Carl Sandburg to call him a "paid liar." In practice, many current practitioners do not want to lie, but they do not do all of their work "in the open," they *do* attempt to persuade rather than merely inform, and they *do* believe that only a fool speaks frankly about matters which could injure a client.

It is time to recognize more fully the work of another public relations founding father whose early statements are much closer to current reality. The writings of Edward Bernays, who created the expression "public relations counsel" during the 1920's, are worth a second look by practitioners who want to *understand* as well as act. It was Bernays, the nephew of Sigmund Freud, who integrated what had been the publicists' trade with the major intellectual trends of the late nineteenth and early twentieth centuries, particularly Freudianism and Darwinism. It was Bernays during the 1920's who gave public relations practitioners not just a job and a paycheck, but a purpose, that of "manipulating public opinion" (Bernays' expression, used positively) in order to counter "the whimsical forces of life and chance."

Facing Facts Frankly

Many contemporary public relations practitioners do not like to think of themselves as engaged in "manipulation" or, even worse, "propaganda." Many euphemistic words are thrown around in an attempt to avoid such stigmatizing self-identification. But Bernays faced facts frankly in 1928 when he wrote a book on public relations and proudly titled it *Propaganda*. He realized that the pursuit of propaganda is the logical step once belief in a God sovereign over human activities is no longer present. "How can you blame the intelligent business man who has millions invested in his industry, and thousands depend on it for jobs," Bernays asked *Atlantic* magazine readers in 1932, "if he attempts by intelligent propaganda to give these shifting tides of taste a direction which he can follow without loss; to control by means of propaganda what otherwise would be controlled disastrously by chance?"

Bernays not only went beyond Ivy Lee in developing the

rationale for a public relations style which prized manipulation, but also developed a new methodology. A sound practitioner, Bernays wrote, "takes account not merely of the individual, nor even of the mass mind alone, but also and especially of the anatomy of society, with its interlocking group formations and loyalties." The individual is "a cell organized into the social unit. Touch a nerve at a sensitive spot and you get an automatic response from certain specific members of the organism."

The mechanistic nature of this procedure was, for Bernays, no exaggeration. Whether or not he and others could manipulate so precisely was and is open to question, but Bernays claimed that he could "effect some change in public opinion with a fair degree of accuracy by operating a certain mechanism, just as the motorist can regulate the speed of his car by manipulating the flow of gasoline." The way to that goal was through working on the leaders, and through them their followers: "If you can influence the leaders, either with or without their conscious cooperation, you automatically influence the group which they sway."

What Bernays proposed in *Propaganda,* and proudly argued in an *American Journal of Sociology* article entitled "Manipulating Public Opinion," was nothing less than a new way of looking at public relations; while Lee talked about providing "public information," Bernays' goal was to make a hero of "the special pleader who seeks to create public acceptance for a particular idea or commodity." Public relations, for Bernays, no longer needed to be defended as what sinful men do in a sinful society. Public relations would now be proclaimed as the service which saviors of that sinful society would take upon themselves to perform. It was hard work to be continuously "regimenting the public mind every bit as much as an army regiments the bodies of its soldiers," but someone had to do it.

The Behind-the-Scenes Specialist
Who? Bernays' vision of the future of public relations was most

attractive to practitioners trying to rise above publicist status. Certainly, Bernays wrote, "There are invisible rulers who control the destinies of millions." But those were not the political leaders or big businessmen of common paranoia. No, Bernays insisted that, "It is not generally realized to what extent the words and actions of our most influential public men are dictated by shrewd persons operating behind the scenes." The behind-the-scenes operators were necessary to the operation of a society, and there would not be that many of them: "The invisible government tends to be concentrated in the hands of the few because of the expense of manipulating the social machinery which controls the opinions and habits of the masses. ..." As to the job description and title of the behind-the-scenes operators, Bernays was precise: "There is an increasing tendency to concentrate the functions of propaganda in the hands of the propaganda specialist. This specialist is more and more assuming a distinct place and function in our national life. [He] has come to be known by the name of 'public relations counsel.'"

Bernays began *Propaganda,* the most important of his many books, with the assertion that, "The conscious and intelligent manipulation of the organized habits and opinions of the masses is an important element in democratic society. Those who manipulate this unseen mechanism of society constitute an invisible government which is the true ruling power of our country." That was an awesome opening note. Since a democratic society is normally considered to be one in which "the people" in general do rule, and an authoritarian society is often considered one in which a small group of people rule, Bernays was trying to square the circle by arguing, in effect, that we must kill democracy to save it.

Others during the 1920's argued similarly but were not audacious enough to consider such a degree of social control "democratic." Bernays, though, considered behind-the-scenes manipulation the type of "democracy" that was still practical: "We are governed, our minds are molded, our tastes formed, our ideas suggested, largely by men we have never heard of. This is a logical result of the way in which our democratic society is organized. Vast numbers of human beings must cooperate in this manner if they are to live together as a smoothly functioning society."

Bernays did not stop there; he contended repeatedly that such a behind-the-scenes system is the *only* one possible in a large-scale society which chooses to avoid outright authoritarian control: "Whatever attitude one chooses to take toward this condition, it remains a fact that in almost every act of our daily lives, whether in the sphere of politics or business, in our social conduct or our ethical thinking, we are dominated by the relatively small number of persons—a trifling fraction of our hundred and twenty million—who understand the mental processes and social patterns of the masses. It is they who pull the wires which control the public mind. ..."

Open Competition

Bernays argued that an authoritarian system of control could be preferable to such a "democratic" system: "It might be better to have, instead of propaganda and special pleading, committees of wise men who would choose our rulers, dictate our conduct, private and public, and decide upon the best types of clothes for us to wear and the best kinds of food for us to eat." But this was not going to happen. He wrote: "We have chosen the opposite method, that of open competition. We must find a way to make free competition function with reasonable smoothness. To achieve this, society has consented to permit free competition to be organized by leadership and propaganda." Bernays, once again, did not pull his punches; although some would have hesitated at using "free competition" side by side with certain activities which might appear to favor the opposite of freedom, Bernays rushed in.

This was not to say that Bernays was sanguine about all of these developments. He wrote that, "The instruments by which public opinion is organized and focused may be misused." He noted that "Some of the phenomena of this process are criticized—the manipulation of news, the inflation of personality, and the general ballyhoo by which politicians and commercial products and social ideas are brought to the consciousness of the masses." But Bernays, following the logic of his beliefs, argued that there was no choice: "Such organization and focusing are necessary to orderly life."

Many with the title "public relations counsel," then and now, did not and do not enjoy being called "propaganda specialists." Bernays, though, always put propaganda in the context of his Freud-based beliefs that irrational man possessed a "rubber stamp" mind which had to be stamped with control and civilization before chaos took over, as it rapidly could. The magazine writer Stuart Chase was sarcastic, writing that, "Not only God but Counsels of Public Relations are masters of the mystic pulls of gravitation," but Bernays argued that practitioners would be "socially responsible" *only* if they subordinated individual behavior and conscience to the demand for "manipulating public opinion to prevent chaos."

Public relations practitioners are now the recipients of wide abuse. They are said to engage in "manipulation" for no reason except their own comfort and their clients' benefit. Bernays, though, saw the wider role of public relations in a confused civilization. Current practitioners should study his work so that they may embrace it and extend their awareness of the deeper meaning of what they do, or reject it and reach for alternatives.

Winter 1984

Dr. Marvin Olasky, professor in the journalism department, The University of Texas at Austin.